13

SPIRITUAL FORMATION
for
CHRISTIAN LEADERS

SPIRITUAL FORMATION *for* CHRISTIAN LEADERS

DONALD DEMARAY
REGINALD JOHNSON

Abingdon Press
Nashville

SPIRITUAL FORMATION FOR CHRISTIAN LEADERS

Copyright © 2007 by Abingdon Press

All rights reserved.

This book is printed on acid-free paper.

Library of Congress Cataloging-in-Publication Data

Demaray, Donald E.
  Spiritual formation for Christian leaders / Donald Demaray and Reginald Johnson.
    p. cm.
  ISBN-13: 978-0-687-49504-7 (binding: pbk., lay-flat : alk. paper)
  1. Christian leadership.   2. Spiritual formation.   I. Johnson, Reginald.   II. Title.

  BV652.1.D45 2007
  248.8'92—dc22

                                                                                            2006032835

07 08 09 10 11 12 13 14 15 16—10 9 8 7 6 5 4 3 2 1
MANUFACTURED IN THE UNITED STATES OF AMERICA

CONTENTS

ACKNOWLEDGMENTS

We want to express gratitude to the following who helped with research and writing, and who affirmed and encouraged us in doing the project.

John F. Kutsko, Director of Academic and Professional Resources, Abingdon Press, responded to our book proposal with both enthusiasm and valuable guidance.

Kathy Armistead, also of Abingdon, did careful editing in an affirming spirit.

Our wives, Jo Johnson and Kathleen Demaray, invested time, energy, and expertise in very helpful critiquing.

Kathleen Davenport-Cobble, medical student at the University of Florida, Tampa, examined the chapter on healing and provided useful comment.

David, J. T., and Ruth Seamands, longtime coworkers with Stanley Jones in India, enriched our understanding of the man and his ministry.

Sam Kamaleson, pastor from India and evangelist with World Vision, and longtime friend of Jones, gave helpful counsel in the early stages of our work.

Kathryn Hendershot, doctoral student at Asbury Theological Seminary, did her thesis on Mabel Lossing Jones, the wife of E. Stanley Jones. Kathryn generously shared her findings.

Grace Yoder, Archivist at the Asbury Theological Seminary Library, made the papers of E. Stanley Jones available to us.

Tess Allan, able secretary, assisted with documentation and putting the manuscript into final form.

And Martha Kirkpatrick read the chapter on disciplines and provided very good counsel.

PREFACE

Spiritual Formation for Christian Leaders promises help for growing in Christ. Illustrated from the life and teachings of E. Stanley Jones, late missionary to India and world evangelist, our book takes the reader forward step by step. And every step forward enriches relationships with God, others, and self—requisites for Christian leaders-in-the-making.

Take, for example, a bit of material from Dr. Jones's autobiography, *A Song of Ascents* (Nashville: Abingdon Press, 1968). The following slice of his book tells us instantly that his roots go deep, and it draws us powerfully into the world of spiritual realities.

The Life of Prayer

> When someone asked me what was the secret of my life, I have replied: "If there is anything secret, then it is perhaps in this: First, I have kept up my prayer life daily. So I do not face life alone. My little loaves and fishes in my hands are very inadequate; but in his hands, surrendered to him, they have been adequate to feed the hungry multitudes I have faced around the world, with something left over for others to use."

My Inadequacy, God's Adequacy

> Second, I've always had a task that I couldn't do; it was always beyond me. So I've had to depend on grace. My verse: "In Him who strengthens me, I am able for anything" (Phil. 4:13 Moffatt). "In Him"—not in me; "who strengthens me"—he

doesn't do everything; he "strengthens me." So I can do them by his grace and power: "I am able for anything."

Divine Enablement

"Able for anything"—my motto. I repeat it to myself again and again and again. And I repeat it as the years come and go: "I am able for anything"—anything he calls me to do. For his calls are his enablements. "Without him, not one step over the threshold; with him, anywhere."

At Any Age

So at my age I have almost exactly the same program I had at forty-three. My program: six months in America and six months in the rest of the world, mostly in the East, particularly in India, spent in evangelistic meetings and Ashrams, traveling all the time and writing books in-between daily local engagements.

Not Fussily Trying to Achieve

Secret? This: "Anyone who enters God's rest, rests from his own work as God did from his" (Heb. 4:11 NEB). By full surrender to God, once and for all, and continuous daily surrender, you enter "God's rest." Then you rest from your own works, you are not fussily trying to achieve, you surrender and receive, you are "poor" enough to receive, so the "Kingdom of God is yours"—all its resources yours for the asking and taking. You work effortlessly, without strain and without drain. You enter God's creative "rest." You cease from your "own works" and watch God work through you.

(All quotations above are from pp. 361–62)

What a model! Jones puts the bar high enough to inspire us to reach and search. Clearly he discovered the secrets and encourages us to find them for ourselves.

We do not pretend to explore all the secrets in our book, nor have we simply repeated Dr. Jones. We do address key classical concerns, but in modern-day categories, pictures, and language. In addition, we would like to think that in nine brief chapters you will find help to put your own roots down deeper and God's power to liberate you to ministry. Precisely that makes his servants both contagious (one of Brother Stanley's favorite words) and authoritative in leadership.

DON DEMARAY

REG JOHNSON

I. CAN I REALLY EXPERIENCE TRANSFORMATION?

Conversion was the pivot on which everything turned in my life. (A Song of Ascents)

Seventy-nine percent of Americans polled describe themselves as "spiritual," reported a *Newsweek* study (29 August–5 September 2005, p. 50). This "impulse to seek communion with the Divine," as their reporter phrased it, is the heart of the spiritual quest (ibid., p. 50). People want a personal relationship with God that will lift them from their mundane life and give them a life with deeper meaning and richer dimensions. Is that possible?

The Christian answer is an emphatic yes. The answer is based not upon our ability to "find" God, but upon the realization that God has found us. Receiving and living in that good news changes everything.

A CASE STUDY

Stanley Jones, born in Baltimore, Maryland, on January 3, 1884, was raised in a home that was heavy on rules and light on grace. Empty and directionless in his teen years, he came to the conclusion that rebelling had not supplied what was missing in his life.

Seventeen was his turning point age. The local Methodist church was hosting a guest speaker. Brother Stanley showed up for the first couple of services and was touched by what he heard. But by the third day, he felt desperate for God. That afternoon he

1

knelt and prayed by his bedside. "O Jesus, save me tonight." Hope stirred, and he sensed he was on the verge of something momentous. It was actually better than he imagined. His simple and sincere prayer had already opened the door to God, who was stirring him awake. "God," as he liked to say, "is only one short step away from any of us." The simplest prayer—"Yes" or "Help"—is all that is needed. It can change everything.

When the pastor gave an opportunity to respond at the end of the evangelistic service, Brother Stanley was the first to the altar. As he went to his knees, he realized that God was already there, welcoming him. He grabbed the man next to him and exclaimed, "I've got it!" In his autobiography he explains: "I had him—Jesus—and he had me. We had each other. I belonged. My estrangement, my sense of orphanage were gone. I was reconciled" (*A Song of Ascents* [Nashville: Abingdon Press, 1968], p. 28).

Jones's direct experience of God launched an adventure of a lifetime. "Life began there. Note I say 'began'—the whole of my life has been an unfolding of what was infolded in that moment" (ibid, p. 28). Because of his sense of always being "in-process," Brother Stanley never called himself a Christian. Such a word had a ring of finality that didn't match the dynamic reality of his experience. Until his dying day he referred to himself as "a Christian-in-the-making."

What can we learn from Stanley Jones about spiritual transformation?

JESUS

The starting point for spiritual transformation isn't the subject of God. If it were, we would debate endlessly about which version of God to accept. Neither do we begin with the human creature; for if we did, we would start and likely remain stuck there. Instead, the place to begin is with the God-man, Jesus Christ. Says Brother Stanley, "If I were to put my finger on the most important verse in Scripture, I would unhesitatingly put my finger on this one: 'And the Word became flesh'" (*The Word Became Flesh* [Nashville: Abingdon Press, 1963], p. 3).

Amid a sea of spiritual options, this is the fundamental truth upon which true Christian spirituality builds: we live on a visited planet. Other great religions emphasize a philosophy of life, moral teachings, spiritual discipline, or techniques. In those cases you might say that the Word becomes words. The sacred writings of other faiths may promote noble values but are presented as mere ideas. By contrast, Christianity focuses on Jesus. It announces the appearance of a flesh and blood person who perfectly embodied his own teachings, actually forgave his enemies, and willingly offered himself on a cross (see, for example, *Word Made Flesh*, p. 48).

Jesus did more than merely live what he taught; his claims about himself make that clear. He professed a unique relationship with his Father who had sent him from heaven to reveal God's true nature and to save the lost. Just here is where Christian spirituality begins. What distinguishes the Christian faith from other spiritual options is not that its ideas are better. What makes Christianity distinctive is that although other approaches deal with the human quest for God, the Christian gospel tells the story of God's search for human beings. God's pursuit resulted in the Word (God's self-communication) becoming flesh. Jesus is God's personal approach to us from the unseen realm. In Jesus, God made himself understandable and lovable to us. Once Jones responded to a woman who thought God to be distant with the question: "Could you love a God who has a face like Jesus?" (*A Song of Ascents*, p. 31).

In later years, Jones lamented that too many students graduate from our schools of theology with little to share except high-minded ideals or a philosophy of life. They lack the conviction of having "good news" to announce (*Word Became Flesh*, p. 5). "You go throughout the world preaching," a TV interviewer once quipped to Jones. "What do you have to preach that others do not have?" Jones's reply was simple and to the point: "I have Jesus Christ—the Word become flesh" (ibid., p. 6). Brother Stanley always saw his role as that of a witness, speaking from firsthand

3

experience of this reality. He did so with the relaxed assurance that he didn't need to defend Jesus but simply to announce what God had done for us humans by coming to us in the flesh. He was confident that God's Spirit would take care of the rest.

David Seamands, former missionary to India, once told me about going with Jones to a university where he was to present an open lecture, followed by a question-and-answer period. A huge crowd of professors, lawyers, and students gathered to hear him. When he announced his subject, conversion, Seamands said that his own heart sank. The word "conversion" had a very negative connotation in India. It was associated with proselytizing, a hated practice in that country.

The largely hostile audience listened, stone-faced, as Jones lectured brilliantly for over an hour. When the time came for questions, one academic leader stood and said bluntly, "Let me see if I understand what you are saying, Dr. Jones. Are you saying that you want to convert me to Jesus? Is that what you're saying? Is that why you've come here?" To which Jones responded: "That's exactly what I'm trying to do. But please, promise me this: if you ever find someone who is greater than Jesus, will you please come and try to convert me to that person?" Jones's message wasn't Christianity, but the person, Jesus Christ. Jesus had captured his heart.

His Cross

Here's the second thing Brother Stanley teaches us about spiritual transformation. When Jesus came to earth, he not only showed us the human face of God, but also revealed God's diagnosis and cure for our condition: we are lost and perishing, but Jesus came to save us. "This is how much God loved the world: He gave his Son, his one and only Son. And this is why: so that no one need be destroyed; by believing in him, anyone can have a whole and lasting life. God didn't go to all the trouble of sending his Son merely to point an accusing finger, telling the world how bad it was. He came to help, to put the world right again" (John 3:16-17 *Message*).

Those compact words summarize the Great Saga. God gave us humans the gift of freedom. That means that we are free to love him; he will not force us. The choice is always ours. Of course we can choose to live without regard for God. We can have the attitude, "I am free! I can do anything that I want to do." But placing ourselves at the center results in brokenness and hurt. We reap the consequences of our poor choices. Destruction of human life and happiness is not something God imposes from outside, but results from living "against the grain" of God's intention. The universe will not endorse a life lived in contradiction to its original design and purpose.

Jesus couldn't have described it more poignantly: it broke God's heart to see us perishing in self-defeat. When he saw the world spinning out of control and the lives of his human creatures in disarray, he suffered the pain that a parent feels for his or her prodigal, estranged child. God came alongside his broken, wayward, and wounded loved ones. Brother Stanley interpreted John's depiction of Jesus as the "Lamb slain from the foundation of the world" (Revelation 13:8 KJV) to mean that from the very beginning there was a cross, etched into the Father's heart. From that perspective, Jesus' crucifixion made visible what had been invisible, and therefore unrecognized by the human species. The "outward cross that was lifted up in history is a sign of that inward cross that lies upon the heart of God" (*Christ and Human Suffering* [London: Hodder and Stoughton Ltd., 1933], p. 168).

Jesus was willing to go through all the hate and evil in the world in order to win back those whom God loved so dearly. If dying was the only way to put the world right again, then he would choose death. Imagine the implications! At the heart of the universe is self-sacrificing love. When Jesus bore our sins on the cross, he revealed the depths of God's love by making things right between us. The cross is both reconciliation and a revelation (*Conversion* [New York: Abingdon Press, 1959], p. 69).

God's breathtaking gift confronts us with serious choices, and we are never really finished with them.

5

- Will we continue letting others define our worth, or accept God's assessment of our value?
- Will we cling to our notion that God's favor must be earned, or embrace grace as his gift?
- Will we continue as if our lives were our own to spend, or realize that we are God's and place ourselves in his hands?

In many ways, the last question is the most basic, encompassing all the rest. "You also are among those who are called to belong to Jesus Christ," writes Paul (Romans 1:6 NIV). It is our choice whether we will respond to this call, and choose to live, and continue living, from this new "focused center" of Jesus' cross (2 Corinthians 5:15 *Message*).

His Kingdom

When we pull the roots of our lives from the soil of self-centeredness and transplant them into Christ, we begin living in a new environment: the kingdom of God (*In Christ* [New York: Abingdon Press, 1961]). In this new "ecological system," we interact with God who is present and active, and we live interdependently with other Christ followers, whom he calls his "body" on earth. Together, we are living under God's direction and influence.

What happens when we live in God's governing presence?

- We learn to trust Jesus in the little and big things that we face.
- Jesus is our teacher of how to live so we study his words in order to apply what he says.
- Regardless of where we are or what we are doing, fulfilling God's plan is our ultimate objective and purpose.
- We pray and we live for his Kingdom to come and his love to be done on earth, as it is in heaven.
- Our prayers include listening for what God wants us to do and then following through on the ideas that he gives to us.

- We approach each day as if we are "on assignment," as if we are God's agents who are under his direction.
- We are not left to accomplish our mission alone but are interconnected with companions through whom we discover God's sustenance and strength as we worship, work, and journey together.

SPIRITUAL REBIRTH

Nicodemus's story, recorded in John 3, is familiar. This conscientious Pharisee didn't want to displease God or fail those who looked to him as a leader. He had seen Jesus, heard what he had to say, and perhaps even admired him. Even though showing interest in this Nazarene could cost him his reputation, perhaps even his job, he was drawn to Jesus, compelled to find out more. So he made an appointment, and, in the evening shadows, he made his way to the place where Jesus was staying.

After exchanging pleasantries, Nicodemus came right to the point. "Rabbi, we know that you are a teacher who has come from God; for no one can do these signs that you do apart from the presence of God" (John 3:2). Don't you wonder what Jesus heard beneath those words? Admiration? Appreciation? Confusion? Yearning? Wonder?

Jesus' response was frank and to the point. "Nicodemus, here is a fundamental spiritual law: no one can see the kingdom of God without being born from above" (v. 3, paraphrase).

"How can a person be born when he is old?" Nicodemus asked, perhaps referring to the ancient heritage and tradition in which he was embedded. Jesus responded that unless he was born of water and the Spirit, he could never enter the Kingdom (v. 5). In other words, Nicodemus must acknowledge his spiritual impoverishment and utter dependence upon God's grace just like some God-fearing Gentile going down into the water for initiation into the Kingdom. Nicodemus had assumed that he was already "in" the kingdom of God by virtue of pedigree and performance, but Jesus was showing this spiritual leader the necessity of spiritual rebirth.

The stirring of an evening breeze became a ready metaphor for the Spirit's mysterious activity and influence. Nicodemus hadn't realized it, but it was the Spirit who had attracted him to Jesus that evening. Now Nicodemus needed to look up to Jesus as God's gift who had been sent down to earth, the one to whom the Spirit has brought him.

God is endlessly creative. No two humans have exactly the same story about how they discover or receive God's unconditional love. However, every person, without exception, regardless of status or education or ethnicity, is awakened by the initiative of grace, to which they can choose to respond.

The sense of being disconnected and orphaned that haunts us, added to the yearning for direct experience with God, is actually the pressure of God's hand on us. Our spiritual quest is an expression of an unfilled capacity for "something more" that is implanted by God who synchronizes it with his search for us. Our longings are actually God's nudges. Just as we can grasp neither the origins nor the destination of an evening breeze, neither will we fully comprehend the mysteries of how the Spirit stirs our longings, convicts us of our sins, and draws us to Jesus in order to fill and empower our lives.

"Spiritual transformation," "new birth," and "conversion" all point to the fact that a person can begin again. We have the power to choose whether we will make Jesus the center of our lives or whether he will be just one among our many interests. To be honest, Jesus can be displaced from his proper place even in his most devoted followers, and it can happen so gradually that they hardly notice. Those of us who are in professional ministry have our own special challenges in this regard. Words and concepts can become our substitutes for vital relationship with the living Christ. Our seemingly endless activity of "doing" for him may replace "being" in him and with him. We may treat Scripture as only a professional tool for preparing sermons, so that it ceases to be a source for prayer and a place to listen for

God's personal communication with us. When we wander like that, how do we find our way back?

FINDING OUR WAY HOME AGAIN

In his little classic *Abundant Living* ([New York: Abingdon-Cokesbury Press, 1942], pp. 22–28), Jones offers a kind of map for making connection with God and "doing life" with him. It is a helpful prayer guide for anyone wanting to return to Christ and reinstate him at the center of life.

- *Review your life*. Honest appraisal is essential. Is there evidence that your life has become essentially self-referenced? Has your focus shifted to your own success, possessions, ambitions, resentments, happiness, and so on? Do you sense your spiritual impoverishment?
- *Change directions*. Until the center of our life shifts, our changes are only cosmetic. We must be willing to repent, to change our whole approach and strategy for living. "Anyone who intends to come with me has to let me lead. You're not in the driver's seat; *I* am" (Mark 8:34-35 *Message*). That means that our *turning* is actually a *returning* to our true home in Christ.
- *Shift perspective*. Look at your life from Christ's vantage point rather than from your own. Ask for his help in dropping any attitudes or actions that conflict with his Spirit. Put things right wherever you can. Ask others' forgiveness wherever it is called for. Do the good things God asks you to do.
- *Receive grace*. This is a simple act of trust. You have done what he asked, and now you trust him to do as he has promised. He promises to accept, to forgive, and to dwell in you. Fill your thoughts with affirmations that you receive his life, his light, and his love. Live in the flow of grace. Abiding in him is the key life-change. In fact, life-change is really "life-exchange" since we are allowing him to live his life through us.

- *Renew relationships.* Reenter your relationships with Christ at the center of your life. Here are some of the apostle Paul's reflections on what this will look like (taken from Romans 12:9-20 Message):

  ☐ "Love from the center of who you are; don't fake it. . . .
  ☐ Be good friends who love deeply.
  ☐ Practice playing second fiddle.
  ☐ Don't burn out; keep yourselves fueled and aflame.
  ☐ Be alert servants of the Master, cheerfully expectant.
  ☐ Don't quit in hard times; pray all the harder.
  ☐ Help needy Christians.
  ☐ Be inventive in hospitality.
  ☐ Bless your enemies.
  ☐ Laugh with your happy friends when they're happy.
  ☐ Share tears when they're down.
  ☐ Get along with each other.
  ☐ Don't be stuck-up.
  ☐ Make friends with nobodies.
  ☐ Don't be the great somebody.
  ☐ Don't hit back.
  ☐ Discover beauty in everyone.
  ☐ If you've got it in you, get along with everybody.
  ☐ Don't insist on getting even; that's not for you to do.
  ☐ If you see your enemy hungry, go buy that person lunch.
  ☐ If he's thirsty, get him a drink.
  ☐ Don't let evil get the best of you; get the best of evil by doing good."

- *Make room for God.* Spend some quiet, focused time with Jesus every day. Pray simply and honestly. Bring people and situations to him. Make listening a part of your praying. Meditate on Scripture. Trust that his Spirit is within you, and allow him to be your guide.
- *Put your life in his hands.* Release your fears and surrender yourself to him for whatever he asks you to do. Reframe the way you look at life. "I have been crucified with Christ. My

ego is no longer central. It is no longer important that I appear righteous before you or have your good opinion, and I am no longer driven to impress God. Christ lives in me. The life you see me living is not 'mine,' but it is lived by faith in the Son of God, who loved me and gave himself for me" (Galatians 2:20 *Message*). We can face life's changes, aging, and even death in a different frame of mind now. Keep reminding yourself: "I can make it through anything in the One who makes me who I am" (Philippians 4:13 *Message*).

QUESTIONS

1. Group members can share with one another stories about how they remember first embracing God's unconditional love.
2. Discuss the notion that "the Word made flesh" is the beginning point for Christian spiritual formation.
3. Artists of all genres have sought to express the mystery of the cross and God's redemptive love. Share a poem, hymn, painting, or a story that has been especially meaningful for you.
4. Discuss characteristics of the "new environment" of the Kingdom into which we have stepped by deciding to follow Jesus.
5. What are signs of "soul erosion" that you have found in your own life, and how have you experienced God's grace calling you back "home" again?

II. Really, Abundant Life?

From first to last, the Christian faith is a religion of the Spirit. (The Way to Power and Poise)

A small picture rests on my desk: five loaves and two fish in a simple basket. It is a reproduction of a mosaic from a fifth-century church that stood on the eastern shore of the Sea of Galilee. It serves as a reminder: God multiplies resources that are offered to him. Have confidence in his compassion and place yourself in his hands.

Stanley Jones learned this lesson the hard way. His assignments had increased exponentially. He was only thirty-two years old when he became superintendent of Methodist churches scattered over a vast territory of four districts in northeastern India, servicing an area of several millions of people. The travel alone was exhausting. In addition, he was in charge of a publishing house with five hundred employees. As his wife put it, Brother Stanley was living like a "chased rabbit" (Letter to "Miss Nellie," his spiritual mother, 21 October 1915).

His situation darkened when his appendix ruptured but was inoperable because of adhesions and infection. Lockjaw set in. He was physically broken and emotionally spent.

It is tempting to emphasize the outer psychological and physical aspects of Jones's ordeal and miss what he later realized as the underlying cause: he faced a spiritual crisis. Can people pastor themselves? Can they go deeper into God's love or discern his presence more clearly without the support of community? Brother Stanley's problem was that he was trying to be his own encourager. The only spiritual teachings he heard were his own, and they were feeble attempts to communicate the most elementary theology in a language that he was struggling to learn. Brother Stanley was spiritually malnourished.

He was offered an early furlough. On the voyage home he was invited to preach at the Sunday worship service. He tried to bring a message about contentment in the midst of calamity using Paul's great words, "I can do all things through [Christ] who strengthens me" (Philippians 4:13). About the time he reached the middle of his sermon, his mind went blank. He closed his notes and sat down in defeated silence, overwhelmed by the profound contradiction: he was preaching beyond his experience.

A year of furlough was not enough to restore his soul and bring balance to his life. He returned to India in a tailspin, emotionally, physically, and spiritually.

In his darkest hour, Providence brought him to the Central Methodist Church in Lucknow, India, to a special evangelistic service. When the meeting ended, he knelt at the altar to pray for others when the still small Voice addressed him: "Are you yourself ready for the work to which I have called you?" Nothing compares to God's questions. They are always simple and always cut to the core issues.

"No, Lord, I'm done for," whispered Jones. "I've reached the end of my resources and I can't go on."

The Divine Physician replied: "If you'll turn that problem over to me and not worry about it, I'll take care of it."

"My eager reply," reported Brother Stanley, "'Lord, I close the bargain right here.' I arose from my knees knowing I was a well man" (*A Song of Ascents* [Nashville: Abingdon Press, 1968], p. 89).

He was almost afraid to tell anyone, for fear that the fresh energy flowing through his body, mind, and spirit would fade. His shattered confidence had been replaced by peace and a deep down assurance that God would provide all he needed for whatever God gave him to do. Jones was back in a conscious communion with the Spirit, surrendering to his control and engaging with him as friend, not just relating to him as an idea. This changed everything: his outlook, his approach to ministry, his disposition, the way he made decisions, and the place he gave to community.

OUTLOOK

Now Brother Stanley realized that everything did not depend on him. It was not that he did nothing; but rather than working for Christ, he rediscovered the principle of allowing Christ to work through him. From this point he always emphasized the order: receive and then respond. Ministry was no longer about proving worth by "successful" performance, but about receiving grace and responding by obedience (*How to Be a Transformed Person* [Nashville: Abingdon Press, 1951], pp. 312–13).

MINISTRY

Jones decided to allow God to run the universe. He no longer felt burdened to protect Jesus or the gospel before a hostile opposition, but eagerly accepted his opportunity to bear witness to what he and others had experienced in Jesus. He saw those to whom he was sent, not as enemies, but as persons with spiritual longing, who were loved by God.

Brother Stanley's confidence in the Spirit empowered him to make deliberate choices that rendered him more vulnerable in his ministry than he had ever dared to be.

- He shifted his focus from the outcasts to the intellectual leaders;
- He moved his evangelistic meetings away from the safety of church buildings and into municipal or university lecture halls; and
- He designed his public presentations so that they moved into dialogue and discussion with critics and seekers.

PRESENCE

Leaning into the Holy Spirit, Brother Stanley worked from a peaceful center. Once a friend commented on how physically exhausted she felt after witnessing Brother Stanley handle a barrage of hostile questioners after one of his evening lectures. Jones reminisced that in earlier days he would have felt the stress of such encounters as acid eating into his soul. Now? Now he was relaxed, even energized by such encounters.

DECISION-MAKING

Early in his new journey in a Spirit-led life, Jones gathered a few others to go with him on a retreat in order to develop a vision statement for his work. The new definition of his ministry provided a lens through which he would discern among the opportunities that were offered in order to clarify how best to focus his work. Confident that God desired a conversational relationship with him, Brother Stanley set aside time each day for his "listening post." He asked, "Lord, what do you have to say to me?" This interaction and dialogue proved to be crucial for creativity, inspiration, and a sense of direction.

COMMUNITY

Since the Holy Spirit dwells in Christ's Body on earth, it was natural that Brother Stanley would look for community as he sought to live by the Spirit. He formed a Christian Ashram at Sat-Tal, in the lowlands of the Himalayas.

In India, "Ashrams" are gatherings of people taking a retreat from their work and other responsibilities in order to spend time with a spiritual teacher, or guru. Jones's visit to Gandhi's Ashram made a profound impression on him. He decided to Christianize this ancient Indian tradition by founding a retreat where Jesus would be the guru and people would gather around him for study, worship, prayer, and sharing in community. The Christian Ashram at Sat-Tal was the first of what became a worldwide retreat movement. Christian Ashrams are the "kingdom of God in miniature," as Jones used to describe them. Racial, cultural, socioeconomic, and denominational barriers come down when Christ is the center of a fellowship of equals. You may want to visit the official site of the Christian Ashram movement to locate an Ashram in your own area (www.christianashram.org/).

Since Brother Stanley's travels made it difficult to have a congregation that he related to in a regular fashion, the Ashram at Sat-Tal was his faith community. Here he shared, prayed, and lived with persons who knew, loved, and were unafraid to critique and challenge one another. It was to this Ashram that he retreated for the months of rehabilitation after the severe stroke he suffered in the last chapter of his life.

In deciding to live by depending on the Spirit, Brother Stanley identified with the path of life that Jesus chose.

FULLY ALIVE

Jesus, fully human and fully divine, did not call upon his unique identity as God's Son as a way of gaining special privileges. Instead, he lived in the same way that he showed us that we could live: in intimate connection and dependence upon the personal presence of the Holy Spirit. By living this way, Jesus is the prototype for what it means to be fully human. Humans may live on earth in communion with God through the Holy Spirit. Jesus prepared his original disciples for his physical absence by promising them that he would ask the Father to send them another friend, a counselor who was the Spirit, to be with them and in them (John 14:16-17). Before his ascension to heaven, Jesus told his followers to wait in Jerusalem because that was where the Father would baptize them with his Spirit (Acts 1:5).

My wife, Jo, and I attended a conference on the Christian life not long ago. On our way home she said, "There is something about that conference that troubles me." I asked her what it was that left her feeling that way. Her answer was striking, "Do you realize that we went through all of those sessions about living as Christians and no one mentioned the Holy Spirit? I have a relationship with all three members of the Trinity: the Father, Jesus, and the Holy Spirit. The Holy Spirit is God present in me. He is my counselor, helper, and constant companion. I cannot live the Christian life without the Spirit."

The disciples would have agreed. Listen to their witness about how the Spirit was indispensable.

- Our authorization for carrying out God's plan of action is "written with Spirit on spirit, his life on our lives" (2 Corinthians 3:8 *Message*).
- We no longer labor under the crushing demand of the law, trying to become acceptable to God; we live in joyous freedom by simply embracing "what the Spirit is doing in us" (Romans 8:4 *Message*).
- "God's Spirit touches our spirits and confirms who we really are. We know who he is, and we know who we are: Father and children" (Romans 8:15-16 *Message*).
- We are given glorious inner strength through the Spirit (Ephesians 3:16).
- As a community of his followers, we are being formed into a dwelling in which God lives by his Spirit (Ephesians 2:22).
- Since we can choose how to live, we choose to live freely, and to live energized and motivated by God's Spirit (Galatians 5:18).
- As we live in this way, the Spirit produces qualities of character, or fruits of the Spirit, in our lives (Galatians 5:22).
- We are empowered to witness to Jesus through the Spirit who has been imparted to us (Acts 1:8).

In the life of Jesus, and in the lives of his followers, from the beginning to the end, it's all about life in the Spirit, who is assuring, companioning, guiding, empowering, interceding, and shaping our lives (*The Way to Power and Poise* [Nashville: Abingdon Press, 1949], p. 33).

THROUGH CRISIS TO DISCOVERY

There is plenty of evidence to back Jones's observation that "the soul gets on by a series of crises" (*A Song of Ascents*, p. 51). Our personal calamities and predicaments often do confront us with our limitations, making us acutely aware of how desperately we need the help of One who is smarter, more loving, and more powerful than we are.

Recently I invited people in a group to write a prayer using this prompt, "Holy Spirit, I especially remember when ..." or "Holy Spirit, thank you for how ..." In every case, notice how the expression of some personal extremity had turned into an experience of spiritual discovery. Here are some of the prayers they shared.

- "You quieted my doubts by filling me with reverent awe before your mysterious, creative presence one starry night."
- "You enfolded me by the physical presence of Christian friends who surrounded me with your love when my parent died."
- "You empowered me when I stepped outside my comfort zone to serve you in a strange new culture by replacing my fears with a peace that could only have come from you."
- "You assured me of God's forgiving and accepting love when I felt that my personal betrayal and failure were beyond pardon."
- "You guided me through a crisis when I knew that I had to let go of someone who was precious to me, and then you created a completely unexpected way of helping fill the hole in my life."
- "You met me as I prayed to you in my worry and confusion and helped me decide on a plan of action that eventually brought resolution."
- "You helped me pray that I would be willing to forgive a person who had hurt me deeply; then you helped me pray for that person to experience your love; and then you helped me

let go of my resentment. I think you're asking me to do something kind, but I haven't been able to cross that bridge yet!"

THE COMPANIONSHIP OF THE HOLY SPIRIT

When I read those prayers for the first time, I was touched by the sense of intimacy and connection they conveyed. They are firsthand experiences of what Jesus promised when he said, "I will talk to the Father, and he'll provide you another Friend so that you will always have someone with you. . . . You know him already because he has been staying with you, and will even be *in* you" (John 14:16-17 *Message*). Jones observed that the first "work" of the Spirit was to be *with* us and *in* us. Whatever gifts we experience are simply the by-products of his presence in us.

The Holy Spirit is a person who cleanses, counsels, guides, empowers, and, most of all, is with us and in us. He comes "alongside" us with all that we need. He strengthens our natural powers and coordinates and focuses them as we surrender to him. He doesn't do everything for us, but reveals the truth to us. "This Friend is the Spirit of Truth," explained Jesus (John 14:16 *Message*). When we live in the truth he reveals, we experience the freedom and peace he offers (*Way to Power and Poise,* pp. 45–46).

Stanley Jones told of how one of his interpreters was tense and anxious that things would go well. Brother Stanley said that he wished he could have gone over to the interpreter, unclenched his tight fists, massaged his overworked soul until it relaxed in peace and trust, and said, "Now let's trust God, he will see us through." Then Brother Stanley referenced the crisis in his own life that I described at the opening of this chapter, saying that in those days he was consumed by the stress and pressure to succeed; but that one day, while he was sitting under an apple tree, God gave him a helpful image. He observed that the fruit of that tree came without effort. God seemed to say to him, "My child, you're tired, aren't you? . . . And you're out of patience." Jones described his response, "I need worry no more about the results. I would simply keep open the channels for Life to flow. Service was no longer a strain, but a joy. And the fruit was now more abundant, for it was not mine, but his" (*Christ at the Round Table* [New York: Grosset & Dunlap, 1928], pp. 177–78).

Such surrender is not weak and tentative. It is not preoccupied with "giving up things," but is about handing over our lives. It is decisive, central, and permanent. After this there are daily surrenders, but this is the big shift that is required for us to be filled with the Spirit and begin living out of the resources of his indwelling presence.

How to Receive the Holy Spirit

How does God impart his Spirit? How can we receive him? Brother Stanley addresses this at the conclusion of his book on the Holy Spirit, *The Christ of Every Road*. He observes that regardless of how much you look, there is no passage in scripture that provides a sequence of steps or a set of techniques for receiving the Spirit. The reason is that the Spirit is not some energy we are attempting to attract, but is a living person to whom we are relating.

When it comes to receiving the Spirit, the real question is how can we fall in love with God? To answer that question, Brother Stanley called upon the analogy of human relationships and how we cultivate love with any person. He observed four essentials: nearness, self-surrender, trust, and what he called "continuous adjustment." His suggestions are very helpful, and what follows is a summary of his thoughts (see *The Christ of Every Road: A Study in Pentecost* [London: Hodder and Stoughton, 1930], pp. 226–38).

(1) *Nearness*. In the story of Pentecost, the disciples spent ten days together, praying—drawing nearer to God. Prayer is God's gift of intimacy with himself. It is an action that leads us into engagement, communion, and connection. Perhaps we have little spiritual effect because our prayers are more about "hunting," trying to get what we want or to get God to do what we think needs to be done, rather than realizing that prayer is about

receiving and making ourselves available to God. To receive God's Spirit we need to spend time with him (ibid., pp. 230–31).

Breathing is a helpful image for prayer. Air surrounds us, presses on us, and seeks entry into our bodies; but we must breathe in order for the oxygen to enter our lungs and sustain our lives. God's surrounding presence is like the air, and prayer is our spiritual respiration. As we pray, we receive God's Spirit into our hearts. Prayer is indispensable for the soul (see O. Hallesby, *Prayer* [Minneapolis: Augsburg Publishing House, 1931], pp. 11–12).

(2) *Self-surrender.* How can love grow unless we are willing to make room for the other person in our life? It is difficult to deepen a relationship if we are preoccupied with our own dreams and if our own plans, involvements, interests, and possessions consume our energies. This is certainly true in terms of our relationship with God. Intimacy with Christ cannot grow so long as we keep him on the margins. So long as anything else has a hold on us, it means that Christ is not at the center. The only way this can be addressed is through the process of detaching, letting go, or surrendering.

When our life revolves around Christ, we ask how he wants us to invest our time, how much money we can donate and to what cause, what are his priorities, and so on. In other words, we are trusting that he knows what is best and that he will lead us in ways that are good for us and for his Kingdom. "When he becomes Lord of all he offers us all. It is only empty hands that can grasp a whole Christ. When we are sure we are withholding nothing we may be sure that God is withholding nothing. The Gift of the Spirit may then become ours" (*Christ of Every Road*, p. 231). To receive God's presence, we realize that half-heartedness simply won't do. We decide to live out the prayer, "I am no longer mine, but yours."

(3) *Trust.* When we step out in surrender, willing to do whatever God may ask, we are expressing trust and confidence in him. Brother Stanley likened it to closing an electrical circuit. Faith or trust is the medium through which human and divine are fused (ibid., p. 228).

Life is filled with opportunities to step forward in the faith that God, who has brought us thus far, will certainly not abandon us now. Sometimes we may feel fearful because of what seem to be the impossibilities of our situation. We may feel discouraged, or a sense of shame may cause us to struggle with self-worth. We may experience disorientation and not know which way to turn or what to do next. When those feelings come, God calls us to look up to him and trust that he will provide everything we need in order to do all he asks us to do. As one of my friends puts it, "God wants us to live by what we know, not by how we feel." Difficult challenges, whether they are outside us or within our own minds, are opportunities to practice faith. Jesus promises that "as fruit bearers, whatever you ask the Father in relation to me, he gives you" (John 15:17 *Message*).

(4) *Continuous adjustment.* Earlier we noted that when life crises face us with our impoverishment and vulnerability, they often cause us to reach out, desperate for God's Spirit. We're in trouble and we need help! After the crisis subsides or is resolved, we may be tempted to say, "Thank you for helping me, Lord. But, I'll take it from here." Or, even worse, we might even forget that it was he who accomplished the good results, thinking to ourselves about how well *we* did or how fortunate to others that *we* stepped in and exercised our talents. No longer God-focused, we have reverted to our old patterns of living.

In order to live by the Spirit, we must move from crisis to "continuance," as Brother Stanley put it (*Christ of Every Road,* p. 236). That means we must break from the pattern of only turning to him in emergencies and practice living in his presence throughout the day. Brother Stanley pointed out that when Jesus spoke about the gift of the Spirit in John 7:37, the Greek version uses a verb tense that expresses a completed, but continuous, action; the believer "drinks and keeps on drinking." "Crisis leads to continuance," observed Brother Stanley (*Christ of Every Road,* p. 236). Receiving the Spirit is not "once and done," but a dynamic relationship that is cultivated, grows, and matures as we continue with him. When the act of full surrender turns into a continuous process of letting go, we are allowing the Holy Spirit to carry us like a life-giving current through every aspect of our lives.

This implies that we will be watchful over our hearts because we want to honor God and live only for his glory. We will be spiritually sensitive to any of our motivations, actions, or attitudes that betray how old ego needs have displaced God from the center of our hearts. We not only will be watchful over our hearts, but also will be attentive to God's presence in our lives. We will take the time to review the day for experiences of grace and goodness, rehearsing them in prayer in order to become more appreciative of the Spirit's activity in and around us.

As we practice being present to the Holy Spirit, we are becoming the persons God always intended for us to be: childlike in trust, unpretentious in character, and loving in our intentions. Empowered by God, we are living out of his abundance, not our scarcity, and with a sense of expectancy rather than a sense of apprehension.

Reflecting on his experience of following the leading of the Holy Spirit to India, Brother Stanley put it this way:

> The Inner Voice did not fail me then. It has never failed mesince. In many a crisis, too intimate to spread on the pages of a book, I have looked to Him to give me a clear lead and I would follow. He has never failed to give me that lead sooner or later, and when He has given it, it has always turned out to be right. He has never let me down. I have let Him down, time and again, but I find Him utterly dependable. I am sure that outside of [God's] Will I cannot succeed; inside of [God's] Will I cannot fail. (*Christ of Every Road*, p. 238)

QUESTIONS

1. Write a letter to the Holy Spirit using this prompt: "Holy Spirit, I especially remember when …" or "Holy Spirit, thank you for how …".

2. Think back to the story of Stanley Jones and his interpreter. What words could you say to yourself the next time you realize how tense you are feeling because of some situation you are facing?
3. Turn to the last section of this chapter ("How to Receive the Holy Spirit") and turn the four headings into a prayer guide for a heart-to-heart dialogue with God.

III. Is Christian Community Possible?

The Kingdom of God on earth is the most astonishing and radical proposal ever presented to humanity. It is nothing less than that the whole of life shall be organized around one center—the will of God. (How to Be a Transformed Person)

Imagine a world without countries and without wars. Imagine people sharing so that greed and hunger are things of the past. Imagine all of humanity as a vast brotherhood. "You may say that I'm a dreamer," John Lennon's voice now trailed into the cold night air, "but I'm not the only one. I hope that some day you'll join us and the world will live as one." The camera panned the vast crowd of athletes gathered in the stadium for the opening ceremony of the 2006 Winter Olympics. I hope I never forget the sight, not of uniforms and flags, but of the eyes of young athletes. It was as if so many of them were taken somewhere else in their minds, just for a moment, as if the song awakened a dream.

John Lennon's words touched a haunting, collective memory of an Original Plan that we humans lost somewhere in time and long to recover. We ache for it. Whenever we hear of another roadside bombing in Iraq, see pictures of whole villages starving or the overwhelmed resources of AIDS-ridden hospitals in Africa, or watch a news clip about another act of violence in our community, it stirs in us because we know that we were made better than this.

THE UNSHAKABLE KINGDOM

We were made for the kingdom of God. Since it is written into us, it is strange that we have such difficulty accepting it. Jesus

27

came to establish God's Original Plan, the kingdom of God on earth. But although we accept much of what Jesus said and are filled with devotion before the sight of his cross, we seem to find it difficult to embrace his vision and abandon ourselves to his mission for the world.

It took a trip to Communist Russia in 1934 for Stanley Jones to realize the significance of the kingdom of God. At the time of his trip, the social and economic experiment of Communism was still in its infancy but was already posting impressive results. Brother Stanley witnessed its power to lift the plight of the poor and to inspire the idealism of youth. Communism's ambition was extravagant. It was out to change the world.

Back in his hotel the evening after his first day in Moscow, Jones wondered about all he had seen. He opened his Bible, and the very first words his eyes fell on were these : "Let us be grateful for receiving a kingdom that cannot be shaken" (Hebrews 12:28 RSV). It was as if he were reading the sentence for the very first time. The kingdom of God will not and cannot be shaken. What a contrast to the instability all around him.

Brother Stanley knew that, despite some of the positive gains of Communism, it was bound to collapse. It had to. No movement relying on force to control its people can last. Then he reflected on other options that were being paraded as humanity's hope. He thought of how each was deeply flawed, unable to bear the weight of world transformation.

In a moment of sheer clarity, Jones saw it: everything is ultimately unstable except one thing, the kingdom of God. That is an "absolute" in a world of relativisms. Everything must be reevaluated in relation to the kingdom of God (*The Unshakable Kingdom and the Unchanging Person* [Nashville: Abingdon Press, 1972], p. 33). Our choice is clear, Brother Stanley concluded. Either we enmesh ourselves in atheistic materialism, or we make the kingdom of God central.

THE UNCHANGING CHRIST

The very next morning in his Moscow hotel room, another verse riveted Jones's attention. "Jesus Christ is the same yesterday and today and for ever" (Hebrews 13:8 RSV). What astonishing words. In this world filled with turmoil and flux there is One who is constant and reliable. Jesus is, was, and will always be God's Word made flesh, our Redeemer, God's gift of grace, and the One worthy of being the very center of our life. Jesus doesn't change, thought Brother Stanley, he just keeps "unfolding." The more you see in him, the more you realize there is to be seen.

Those two insights in Moscow were pivotal and became the absolutes on which Brother Stanley's ministry was built: the "Unshakable Kingdom" and the "Unchanging Person," two phrases that became the title of a defining text he published in 1972 (ibid., pp. 33–34).

THE GOLDEN CORD

The Kingdom and the Person are two strands that intertwine into one golden cord. Jesus weaves them together in Matthew 19:12 and 29. He speaks of actions done for the sake of the Kingdom *and* for his own sake, as though they were interchangeable, two sides of the same coin. It is obvious as you look at his life. Jesus did more than announce the coming of a kingdom; he embodied it. What he taught in the Sermon on the Mount were the core values that he had been living out in Nazareth.

Jesus' announcement that "the kingdom of God is at hand" is not a supplement to the good news that God sent his only son to save the world, but a description of what happened when he did. The Kingdom is the natural outflow and expression of Jesus' life. When God walked on earth he reordered the lives of those who surrendered to him. Jesus' description of the Kingdom is what life under his authority looks like. The implication is clear. If Jesus is God made visible, then he has every right to ask us to hand over our lives to him. Nothing else makes sense.

LIFE IS AN ADVENTURE

Life changes when we step into God's kingdom to live under his direction. This is why the "listening post" was such an important spiritual practice for Jones. He knew he needed direction, inspiration, and wisdom, so he spent time every day in silent, listening prayer. He listened because he knew that there was One who was present and who had things to communicate with him. He was hungry for that. When any of us begin to approach life this way, living becomes an adventure. We take time each day to be quiet and receptive, asking: "Lord, is there anything you want me to hear? Is there something you want me to do? Is there someone you want me to talk with?"

God gives us daily assignments. People around us don't normally see what is really happening. They may only notice us taking care of our ordinary responsibilities and handling our everyday relationships. "Nothing extraordinary there," they might think. They just don't get it. On the outside, we may look no different; but actually, as followers of Christ, we approach our daily responsibilities as God's assignments, and the people who cross our paths as those dear to God, whom he brings into our lives. "We make the commonplace a consecrated place," says Jones, "by the spirit which we bring to it" (*How to Be a Transformed Person* [Nashville: Abingdon Press, 1951], p. 288).

GOD USES US TO CHANGE THE WORLD

Kingdom living not only changes how we live our personal lives, but also involves us in transforming the world. The world is becoming a better place not only as individuals live more like Jesus and do their part, but also because God is calling forth a "people" for himself and using them collectively—a positive critical mass—to change the planet.

This collective intention of God is visible in his original covenant with the small nomadic tribe in the ancient near east whom he promised would be his people, and he their God. His purpose was not to make them his "pets," to be treated with favoritism, but as his pattern for all humankind, a "light to the Gentiles," missionaries to the world, carrying the good news that he alone is God and we humans are his people.

The failure of Israel to be faithful to his call is a sad epic, but the unfolding of God's persistent and eternal pursuit is the over-riding theme of Scripture. When the time was right, God sent Jesus. When Jesus embarked on his mission, he gathered people to follow him *together*, in other words, to live with him in community. The fact that there were twelve in his original band was reminiscent of the twelve tribes of Israel. Through Jesus, God was calling forth a "new Israel."

At Pentecost, when the Holy Spirit was given to the whole group gathered in the Upper Room, it was the fulfillment of the ancient promise of the day that would come when "I will pour out my spirit on all flesh" (Joel 2:28). God—whose very presence had once filled Israel's temple, but was withdrawn because of the dis-obedience of his people—was now giving his presence to this body of people who were responding to his grace through Christ. Now he would inhabit not a building but a community that he was fashioning into his new "temple." "Do you not know that you are God's temple and that God's Spirit dwells in you?" Paul asked the believers gathered in Corinth (1 Corinthians 3:16).

The word "church" comes from the Greek word *ekklesia*, which literally means "a calling out" and refers to an assembly or con-gregation of Christians. It is related to another Greek word, *eklektos*, which is used to describe people who are "chosen out" or "selected" by God for service to him. So a church is a gathering of people who have been called out to serve God. As in the days of old, we are not to think of ourselves as God's "pets" or "favorites," but as his missionaries. Jesus makes this very clear in his final words, as recorded in the Gospel of Matthew, in which he sends us out into the world, authorizing and empowering us to make disciples of all nations. He directs us to baptize converts in the name of the Trinity and teach them to obey all that he com-manded. We know that we are not alone. He is with us, in our community, as we embark on our mission (Matthew 28:19-20).

CHRISTIAN COMMUNITY: GIFT OR ACHIEVEMENT?

The title of this chapter, "Is Christian Community Possible?" sounds odd if we are asking whether or not we can make "it" happen because Christian community is not something we can engineer. It is God's gift.

Consider the implications of the images used for those whom Jesus calls out. We are his "Bride," madly in love with him. We are God's "Temple," set aside for him. We are Christ's "Body" composed of members who are carefully fitted, interrelated, and spiritually gifted, all working together for the common good. Jesus gave us his final orders and we are worthy of the name "Church" only if our passion is to do what he has given us to do.

When you travel past farms you sometimes see a sign beside a field that identifies the type of soil or brand of seed that is used in that section of the farm. It is a demonstration plot and shows passersby what they might expect from the application of that same soil enrichment or if they were to plant the same hybrid seed. Every local congregation is to be a kind of test plot, showing the community at large what life under Jesus' lordship looks like. God's intention is nothing less than world transformation, and his plan is to work through us, personally and collectively.

THE CHURCH: A MOBILIZED COMMUNITY

In vivid contrast to twisted human efforts at kingdom building, Jesus' program is for a higher order of life, one based on self-giving love, compassion, goodness, respect, cooperation, and solidarity. It stands in sharp contrast to other approaches that are predicated on exploitation, greed, ethnocentricity, or egocentricity.

In his inaugural message in Nazareth (Luke 4), Jesus described the breathtaking shape of his project for humanity, a vision he drew from Isaiah. In Brother Stanley's reflection on Jesus' words, he laid beside each phrase the population to which we are sent.

- Good news to the poor—the economically disinherited.
- Release to the captives—the socially and politically disinherited.
- The opening of the eyes of the blind—the physically disinherited.
- The setting at liberty the bruised—the morally and spiritually disinherited.
- The Lord's Year of Jubilee—a new beginning on a world scale.
- The Spirit of the Lord upon me—the dynamic behind it all. (*Christ and Communism* [London: Hodder and Stoughton, 1937], pp. 43–44)

Jesus expects us to identify with and, wherever possible, offer our support in places where such efforts are being made. This gives authenticity to our words because we are incarnating Jesus' passion.

What characterizes a church that is engaged with Jesus for social transformation? The following statements are not exhaustive, but certainly point in the right direction. Use them to evaluate your strengths and weaknesses and to invite God to help you identify appropriate strategies of response.

- The Kingdom mission of Jesus gives purpose and direction to our life together.
- We believe, even in the midst of serious social problems, God uses persons to change things.
- We like to help people recognize how God yearns to transform social structures.
- We show generosity as a personal witness to the gospel.
- We practice hospitality to marginalized persons.
- We engage in works of justice and mercy on a regular basis.
- We raise awareness of the social needs around us and intercede, asking God to show us what we are to do.
- We care for the earth and its resources and teach others to do so as well.

- We encourage others to give sacrificially to critical needs in the world.
- We pray about global issues such as injustice, racism, war, poverty, the AIDS epidemic, and so on, and teach our members to do so as well.

LIVING AS DISCIPLES IN A HOSTILE ENVIRONMENT

Jesus knew that it would be impossible for us to sustain Kingdom-focused lives without the support of others. That's why he gave us to one another. Local churches are life-support systems for people who are living and working in a spiritually hostile environment. How could we make it without one another's support?

The sad thing is that our deepest wounds can come at the hands of those who are supposed to be our most faithful encouragers. It was certainly that way for Jones. Hardly a day would pass that he didn't hear from a vicious critic from some quarter of the church. Because of his social and political views, Brother Stanley remained an enigma or a maverick to many, even in his own Methodist denomination.

He found companionship in a small group of soul friends and nourishment in the Christian Ashrams that he founded. Here's an example:

On the evening of August 15, 1963, just before preaching at an Ashram gathering about the transformation of character, Jones read aloud a letter that he had just written to a magazine editor in response to an article published on racism.

In order to put his comments that evening into perspective, I will share a story from his daughter, Eunice Mathews. In a personal letter, she described how her father had not considered his book on Gandhi to be a success but that all of that had changed just a few months earlier. Boston University hosted a banquet in honor of Dr. Martin Luther King Jr., the announced recipient of the Nobel Peace Prize. Eunice and her husband, James K. Mathews, were in a line of persons congratulating Dr. King.

When Dr. King heard her name associated with E. Stanley Jones, he immediately responded: "Wait, I've read many books on Gandhi, but it was not until I read your father's that I saw the power of nonviolence." Eunice shared this with her father in a letter and said that he had been deeply gratified. She continued her story by saying that, years later, she was visiting the King Center in Atlanta. She was making her way through the memorabilia when she came to an upstairs room where Dr. King's copy of her father's book about Gandhi was in a special display of its own. It was opened to page 88, with King's own writing across the top of the page: "This is it!"

With this backgorund, we return to the summer evening in 1963 when Brother Stanley shared with his Ashram family the letter he had just written to a magazine editor. First, Brother Stanley described how he had recently discovered that it was his book on Gandhi that introduced King to nonviolence as an attitude and approach for social change and that when King read about it he knew that it was exactly the powerful instrument that he had been looking for. From now on, he would teach nonviolence as a way of spiritual influence and response wherever there was hatred and prejudice. He saw it as God's preferred way to break down ancient walls of hostility by suffering with grace and showing goodwill toward the oppressor.

Jones continued,

> This made me responsible in a way for what is happening in our country, especially in our southland. I could retreat into the anonymous and let others take the consequential suffering. I cannot do it and live with myself and with God. So I take the responsibility for having introduced the idea to Dr. King while he introduced the method and the movement. I can only express my gratitude that I've had some small part in turning this inevitable movement from violence to nonviolence.
>
> I call this movement inevitable for it is not a local affair; it is a part of a world movement, a part of the social revolution, the uprising of the underprivileged. It has the groundswell of a world revolution behind it. Therefore you cannot stop it: hinder it, but not stop it.

My only regret is that violence has crept into the movement, the Negro retaliating in kind. My appeal to my Negro friends is this: Don't retaliate. You cannot use both methods of violence and non-violence. The violence cancels out the effectiveness of the non-violence. Make it pure non-violence and your movement will be irresistible.

To my white Christian friends of the southland, ally yourself to the future, not to a dying past. The future belongs not to white man, or to colored man, but to man as man. Everyman, regardless of class or color, is a man for whom Christ died. Ally yourself to that and you ally yourself to the future, and you ally yourself to your Christian faith. If not, then you ally yourself to segregation from that faith. There is nothing behind you except your prejudices. Your Christian faith is the one possibility around which both sides can come together on a higher level, on the level of justice and brotherhood. Boldly apply that faith to this issue. Your friend and His, Stanley Jones.

Then Jones added these very candid remarks to his Christian friends:

I'm sending this to a magazine. I don't know where this position is leading me, but I'll have to follow. If it means to take my place alongside of these who are suffering and going to jail, I suppose there is nothing to do but be a part of it. This is a question on which we must take our stand. It is a revolution and we've got to commit ourselves. My son in law, Bishop J. K. Mathews, and I have been talking about this. He has been in a procession in Chicago, allying himself to that side. If we had both been free this summer we would have probably gone in deeper. But my excuse, which I suppose down deep I was glad to have, was that I didn't want to disrupt these Ashrams by stepping out and allying myself to this movement with its consequences. So, when these (Ashrams) are over, I'm not sure what the future holds. At any rate, this is an issue on which we must take our stand. (Author's personal transcription of an audio recording of Stanley's Ashram sermon, "The Transformation of Character," preached on August 15, 1963)

IMAGINATION, INTENTION, IMPLEMENTATION

We started this chapter with John Lennon's lyrics to "Imagine" running through our minds. Stanley Jones had a compelling social vision just like Lennon's vision. The difference was that, for Jones, the vision was centered in and embodied by a person who had commanded his attention and devotion.

Brother Stanley took Jesus' words seriously and sought to follow them and to teach others to do the same. When Jesus spoke of the kingdom of God, Brother Stanley imagined it, thought through the implications, and then found practical ways to implement it. "His objectives were simple," wrote Paul Rees, a well-known preacher and contemporary of Stanley Jones. "To turn the abstract into the concrete, the ideal into the real, the theoretical into the practical, the verbal into the vital, the dreamy future into the dynamic present—this was his consuming desire and purpose" ("E. Stanley Jones: Christ-Intoxicated," in *Transformation* 18, no. 4 [Winter 1983]: p. 24).

His legacy was impressive:

- He sided with Indians in their resistance to British rule.
- He insisted that Ashrams in the United States be multiracial and multidenominational.
- He never flinched when it came to relating a Kingdom perspective to social issues.
- He contributed the proceeds of his book sales to the poor through various church groups and Christian organizations in India, with special interest in house-building and lease-furnishing projects and providing scholarships to help fund professional training for hundreds of young people; but he never drew attention to his own sacrifices.
- He founded the Nur Manzil Psychiatric Center in Lucknow, India, a facility serving in the spirit of Christ those with mental and emotional illness, regardless of their ethnicity or social stratum.

Stanley Jones did more than imagine; he genuinely believed that God's Kingdom vision could be realized, that God chooses to work through humans, that each Ashram and every congregation is to be a microcosm of the Kingdom, and that we can do nothing without God's empowerment. This is the life for which we were made.

QUESTIONS

1. What is the difference between approaching Christian community as a gift we receive, rather than as a goal we achieve?

2. After reading the section, "Life Is an Adventure," what changes will you make in order to increase the "adventure factor" in your own life?

3. What evidence do you have that your congregation embraces God's Kingdom mission? In what areas is growth needed?

4. How do you experience your congregation, or small group, as a "life support system" that sustains you in a spiritually hostile environment?

IV. Does God
Heal Us?

I was suddenly touched in a dark moment, and from that
time I've known health and life. (The Way)

Each of the chapters in this book represents one of nine
major components characteristic of E. Stanley Jones's spirituality. Jones covers healing in depth, answering the question, Does God heal us? in full-spectrum style. God, he says, heals
seven ways: through surgeons, through physicians, through mental suggestion, through climate, through deliverance from negative thoughts, through the direct touch of God's Spirit, and
through the Resurrection (*The Way* [New York: Abindon-
Cokesbury Press, 1946], 260–63).

THROUGH SURGEONS

Kathleen's back hurt badly; at times she crawled from one
room to another. She tried professional massage, chiropractic
treatment, bed rest, positive thinking, and other therapies familiar to her during a long life. She hesitated to visit a surgeon; she
had heard sad tales of unsuccessful back surgeries. But after
earnest prayer, she knew she must see a specialist.

X-rays and an MRI revealed serious problems related to what
the doctors called stenosis (narrowing) of the spinal canal. The
surgeon looked at the pictures and recommended a specific pro-
cedure. Surgery proved totally successful.

Surgical procedures, fine-tuned in our day and increasingly less
invasive, often provide God's answer to physical challenges.
Kathleen wisely asked multiple questions before submitting to
the hospital experience.

Another scenario: this one about a doctor friend who needed surgery, but hesitated to schedule it. How could he take time away from patients? Yet pain challenged his well-being and threatened efficiency. Surgery came off beautifully. "The surgery was done with a scope," he writes. "I went home the same day (Wednesday) and went back to work the next Monday."

Surgery is God's gift, a therapeutic grace. It can transform one's perspective, as it did with Kathleen and my physician friend.

THROUGH PHYSICIANS

Doctors work with a range of options: multiple drug choices, nutrition, exercise therapy, and referrals to specialists. A good general practitioner, seen regularly, knows his or her patients and provides competent guidance. The willingness of both doctor and patient to dialogue looms high on the health agenda. Willingness married to caution, on the part of the patient to experiment, stands high on the agenda too—especially when taking prescription medicines with side effects.

Luke the physician plays an important role in the New Testament. He stands in stalwart profile as a model of healing grace. Not surprisingly, Luke includes physicians in his Gospel (4:23, 5:31, 8:43). Jesus himself, "the Great Physician," signaled "the Way, the Truth, and the Life," unlatching the door to scientific investigation and the grand expanding benefits of medications and treatments (John 14:6). Scholars have documented the seminal role of Jesus in opening the way to research from which we benefit in today's university and laboratory world.

Physicians help us stay well and thus contribute to the well-being of the whole person.

THROUGH MENTAL SUGGESTION

On the one hand, we all know people who meet their health challenges—sometimes formidable ones—with a positive spirit and remarkable vigor: "You can talk health to yourself and it tends to heal" (*The Way*, p. 260). On the other hand, we know people who find the meaning of their lives in tending to their illnesses. They suffer one disease after another and cannot quit talking about physical problems.

Two brothers, brought up in a positive home environment, respond to life differently. The one, with basically good health, complains about every little disease he thinks he has, and often imagines illnesses he does not have; the other, fighting multiple allergies, laughs, gets medical and nutritional help, then goes on with his life, chock-full of activity, virtually unimpeded.

Although psychologists respond to such divergent perceptions of self and life with theories and therapies, the role of spiritual healing merits attention too. Christians, anchoring their faith in God himself and God's grace, condition themselves to astonishing levels of courage and joyful living. This explains Amy Carmichael, an invalid missionary to India, who, with great joy, administered, from her bed, a home for rescued child prostitutes. Her commitment to Christ, renewed daily at Holy Communion, helps explain this remarkable woman. She is a metaphor of countless overcomers (Douglas Houghton, *Amy Carmichael of Dohnavur: The Story of a Lover and Her Beloved* [Fort Washington, Pa.: Christian Literature Crusade, 1988]).

THROUGH CLIMATE

"A change of climate will do you good," the doctor sometimes counsels. And with good reason, given heavy air pollution in some locales, allergens in others, and cold and dampness in still other geographical areas. But haven't you noticed that the climate issue often resides not in geography but in one's attitude? Go to California, Texas, Florida, Colorado—anywhere people come for their health. Notice how many realize little change in health patterns.

Sometimes, however, a new place helps. A pastor and his wife, both suffering a genetic disease that hampers normal breathing, minister in the cold mountains of Switzerland. They must live two or three months annually in Arizona, which restores their health sufficiently to return to the climate that does not suit them year-round. Climate change, coupled with a wonderfully positive faith, extends their lives and service.

Prayerful evaluation must come before moving out of one's present geographical environment. And honest prayer can change one's mental environment.

Through Deliverance from Negative Thoughts

We know from research that fear, loneliness, jealousy, self-preoccupation, jealousy, purposelessness, resentments, guilt feelings—any number of negatives—possess power to produce illnesses.

Martin Seligman, noting that historically psychology has centered in pathology, wondered what would happen if the research and therapy began with positives. Suppose researchers asked such questions as: What makes human beings happy? What factors bring joy and a sense of well-being? Money, education, a high IQ, youth, sun-splashed days? These have only limited power to put us in a good mood. So what does create an upbeat frame of mind? Researchers tell us family, friends, faith, music, prayer, helping someone in need, and exercise—in other words, the positive, wholesome behaviors. (See *Time*, special issue on mind and body, "The Science of Happiness," 12 January 2005.)

We can condition ourselves, by God's grace and personal discipline, to focus on the good rather than on the bad. Positive thoughts and activities telegraph themselves to our bodies, tending to create health. Stanley Jones, ahead of his time, saw this psychosomatic principle clearly; page after page of his published works, along with his public addresses, indicate his remarkable level of insight. His own long life illustrates the psychosomatic principle: he put good things into his mind that passed on to his body in health. Today, we have enormous amounts of scientific data supporting his position (for example, the research of Daniel

Goleman, Redford Williams and Virginia Williams, Harold Koenig, and the John Templeton Foundation scholars). Today, medical schools have lectures on psychosomatic medicine.

What Stanley Jones called the "Twelve Apostles of Ill Health" beckon our attention. *Anger* we now know can cause diseases, including cardiac problems. *Fear* can bring paralysis of mind, even of the body. *Guilt* unresolved, or false guilt brought on by perfectionism, can wilt the spirit and initiate a depressive mind-set. *Self-preoccupation* has power to turn friends away and induce anxiety with accompanying psychological and physical spin-offs. *Worry* can cause panic attacks. *Resentments* have potential for blocking perspective, even suggesting suicidal thoughts. *Control unbridled* (we call dominating people "control freaks") damages our children and threatens fellow workers; the negative reverberations bounce back to the initiator with sometimes drastic consequences. *Sexual activity outside marriage* damages relationships, causing havoc in many directions, emotional and physical. *Jealousy*, the green-eyed dragon, eats at one's inner being. *Stunted creativity* robs us of wholesome outlets and personal fulfillment. *Inferiorities* deprive a person of normal social relationships and produce a cowering posture with its inevitable results. *Lack of love* can make unwanted babies sick, even die, and cause adults to wither emotionally, spiritually, and physically. (See Donald Demaray, *Experiencing Healing and Wholeness: A Journey in Faith* [Indianapolis: Light and Life Communications, 1999], pp. 49–64. The Twelve Apostles of Ill Health are garnered from E. Stanley Jones's writings, such as *Abundant Living* [Nashville: Abingdon Press, 1976].)

What antidotes, what spiritual medicines, have power to counteract these twelve apostles of ill health? Medical research as well as Scripture help counteract these threats common to us all. Take them one by one:

Anger. Redford and Virginia Williams of Duke University demonstrate not only that anger can kill (by cardiac involvement, for example), but also that we can overcome anger. Therapeutic tactics include humor, forgiveness, diversions, and meditation. The Williams's findings relate directly or by suggestion to scripture passages such as Proverbs 29:11 ("A fool gives full vent to his anger, / but a wise man quietly holds it back" [RSV]) or Proverbs 15:18, ("A hot-tempered man stirs up strife, / but he who is slow to anger quiets contention" [RSV]). You will find Eugene Peterson's rendering of Ephesians 4:26 especially helpful: "Go ahead and be angry. You do well to be angry—but don't use your anger as fuel for revenge. And don't stay angry. Don't go to bed angry. Don't give the Devil that kind of foothold in your life" (*Message*). Yes, we ought to get angry at evil—at injustices, for example—but don't let it get the better of you.

Fear. D. Martyn Lloyd-Jones, a doctor (he served the royal family in England) turned gospel minister, observed that fear can cause paralysis (see the story in *Preachers and Preaching* [Grand Rapids: Zondervan, 1971], pp. 37–38). Many of us experience, from time to time, threatening situations in which we feel helpless (for example, before giving a speech); but when fear captures one's mind to cause hormonal changes in the brain, some physical paralysis can ensue. The Bible says a lot about fear. An example is Matthew 6:34: "So don't worry about tomorrow, for tomorrow will bring its own worries. Today's trouble is enough for today" (NLT). Compare that translation with Eugene Peterson's translation: "Give your entire attention to what God is doing right now, and don't get worked up about what may or may not happen tomorrow. God will help you deal with whatever hard things come up when the time comes" (*Message*). Often we see the expression "Fear not" in Scripture—in fact, it is the most frequent pair of words in the Bible. Notice that the angels in the Christmas story begin their addresses to Joseph, Mary, and the shepherds with "Fear not." Clearly, God wants us to know the availability of grace to rob us of unwholesome fears.

Guilt. Harold G. Koenig, Director of Duke University's Center for the Study of Religion/Spirituality and Health, observes the role of forgiveness in releasing one from guilt feelings. The psalmist cries, "For thy name's sake, O LORD, / pardon my guilt, for it is great" (Psalm 25:11 RSV). The Forgiveness Counseling movement in the world of therapy today calls our attention to the profound effects of in-depth forgiveness and helps us work through tough issues. (See, for example, Virginia Todd Holeman, *Reconcilable Differences: Hope and Healing for Troubled Marriages* [Downers Grove, Ill.: InterVarsity Press, 2004].)

Self-preoccupation. Often when Stanley Jones prayed with people for healing, say at a healing service, he said, "Lord, deliver this person from self-preoccupation." He would also counsel, "Once you have given your problem to God, go believing he answered you." Wisely, Dr. Jones knew not all problems yield with such acts; he also knew that our self-induced ailments will go with self-surrender. Jesus declared, "He who finds his life will lose it, and he who loses his life for my sake will find it" (Matthew 10:39 RSV).

Worry. The old English word for "worry" means "strangle." A panicked church member called her pastor; she complained, "I cannot swallow." He visited with her long enough to discover worry in the depths of her being. She expelled her anxieties in talk, then swallowed normally. The Bible has quite a lot to say about worry. Matthew 6:25-34, the famous Sermon on the Mount passage, lets us know our security rests in God himself. St. Paul provides us with excellent therapy: "Don't fret or worry. Instead of worrying, pray. Let petitions and praises shape your worries into prayers, letting God know your concerns. Before you know it, a sense of God's wholeness, everything coming together for good, will come and settle you down. It's wonderful what happens when Christ displaces worry at the center of your life" (Philippians 4:6-7 *Message*).

Resentments. To feel insulted at another's behavior may set up a resentful state of mind. Persisted in, this state of mind can cause havoc, as in the case of the man who divorced his wife because she would not comply with his demands. Sadly, when he did not succeed at making his employees knuckle under, he could no longer tolerate life and committed suicide. Such a power person, who must stand at the top, inevitably sets up in his mind a whole syndrome of negatives. Had the man who took his life instead listened to Jesus—"Make friends quickly with your accuser" (Matthew 5:25 RSV)—he could have avoided esentments. Interestingly, accusation was not his problem;

imagined accusation was. He perceived the lifestyles of his wife and business associates as accusatory.

Control unbridled. Austrian psychiatrist Alfred Adler observed that normal people possess a natural instinct to organize. We set goals, organize plans of action to achieve our aims, then proceed to bring those aims to flower. All well and good. When, however, people overextend the natural organizational instinct, dominance and unbridled control of others result. People who must have their way not only suffer side effects such as resentment, but also document by their behavior that they have an authority problem. In contrast, the Spirit of God graces his children with flexibility, sensitivity to others' perspectives, and the excitement of creative solutions, often solutions no one ever thought of! Notice the authoritative place of Jesus: "Now when Jesus had finished saying these things, the crowds were astounded at his teaching, for he taught them as one having authority, and not as their scribes" (Matthew 7:28-29; compare Matthew 8:9 and 9:6). Notice especially Matthew 28:18: "And Jesus came and said to them, 'All authority in heaven and on earth has been given to me'" (RSV). To surrender to Jesus' authority releases us from the burden of playing God and from the emotional and physical side effects.

Sexual impurity. The seventh commandment stands as a foundation stone of normal, healthy relationships. Sex and family studies reveal that with time faithful monogamous marriages have power to create peace and health in just about every social and personal dimension one can think of. Unfaithfulness has a bad track record. This explains the strong statements of our Lord. Eugene Peterson's rendering of Matthew 5:27-28 makes Jesus' teaching vivid: "You know the next commandment pretty well, too: 'Don't go to bed with another's spouse.' But don't think you've preserved your virtue simply by staying out of bed. Your *heart* can be corrupted by lust even quicker than your *body*. Those leering looks you think nobody notices—they also corrupt" (*Message*).

Face this fact: as in Jesus' day, we live in a lust-saturated culture; only God-graced discipline will save us from promiscuity and adultery and their spin-off social and physical diseases. (Compare Lauren F. Winner, "Sex in the Body of Christ," *Christianity Today* [May 2005]: pp. 28ff., and her book, *Real Sex: The Naked Truth about Chastity* [Grand Rapids: Brazos Press, 2005].)

Jealousy. Shakespeare penned,

> O! beware, my lord, of jealousy;
> It is the green-ey'd monster which doth mock ...
> (*Othello* Act III, Scene 3)

Mock it does! For it exposes our own self-centeredness, and often we put another down to make ourselves look good—which is bad socially as well as personally. No wonder Paul said forthrightly, "Love is not jealous" (1 Corinthians 13:4 RSV). Love does indeed infiltrate one's being, by God's grace, to release us from wanting what someone else possesses.

Stunted creativity. Scientific research tells us that when we absorb ourselves in a creative project—ceramics, stamp collecting, gardening, whatever—chemical activity kicks in to give us that all-over good feeling. Rob yourself of creative opportunities, and find yourself emotionally unfulfilled and frustrated. Reverse that to creative productivity, and find yourself renewed both mentally and physically. God, Creator of the vast universe, made us in his own image (Genesis 1:27); theologians call this the doctrine of *imago dei* (image of God). This explains why we *must* create in order to fulfill our destiny.

Inferiority feelings. Low self-esteem, one of the major challenges of our culture, feeds the psyche with angry thoughts and can actually cause clinical depression. It infects us with social handicaps as well as emotional and physical ailments. Jesus, the master psychotherapist, cuts right across the human conditioning that causes inferiority feelings with his forthright instruction, "You shall love your neighbor as yourself"(Matthew 19:19*b* RSV). By God's grace, we can indeed love and respect ourselves as we love and respect others.

Love deficiency. Just here we come to perhaps the chief cause of disease, emotional, spiritual, and physical; conversely, true love constitutes the supreme medication. Dean Ornish did extensive research on love as therapy (see "How Love Heals," *Reader's Digest* [July 1998], and Ornish's book, *Love & Survival: The Scientific Basis for the Healing Power of Intimacy* [New York: HarperCollins, 1998]). A single example of Dr. Ornish's research illustrates the power of love to heal. He assembled data on 8,500 men: those who said yes to the question, "Does your wife show you her love?" suffered dramatically fewer cardiac problems. First Corinthians 13, the classic love chapter, sites a multiplicity of benefits, and from a specific kind of love: *agape*, the Greek word used throughout that chapter. That kind of love—that self-giving and sacrificial love Jesus demonstrated on the cross, that selfless species of love—telegraphs with enormous power to one's spouse, children, friends, and oneself. *Agape* is supremely therapeutic.

THROUGH THE DIRECT TOUCH OF GOD'S SPIRIT

Saint Augustine, writing early in the fifth century A.D., authored *The City of God* (Harmondsworth: Penguin Books, 1972). In it, he relates personal knowledge of healing miracles: of a blind man (pp. 1034–35), breast cancer (pp. 1037–38), gout (pp. 1038–39), paralysis and hernia (p. 1039), a small boy crushed by a wheel (p. 1042), and so on (Book 22, chapter 8, pp. 1033–47). The final healings, of a brother and sister, recorded in chapter 8, paint a dramatic scene of the pair, terribly sick, now totally restored, standing in Augustine's church service, the whole congregation witnessing the remarkably cured siblings. Commenting on the response of the worshipers, Augustine exclaimed, "They rejoiced in the praises of God with wordless cries, with such a noise that my ears could scarcely endure it" (p. 1047).

Augustine shares his interpretation of these healing miracles. Fervent, believing prayer; strong faith; the powerful witness of the miracle-working God to produce believers out of skeptics—all this and more come into the picture. He sees the value of doctors, grumbles at unbelievers who do not want miracles known, and signals the power of conversion as a healing instrument of the sovereign God.

How many healing miracles have taken place in history, only God knows. Believers often share their divine cures. I can personally witness to hearing hundreds of stories during more than four decades of healing ministry.

Stanley Jones says he has no doubt of the direct touch of God, "I know it. For I was suddenly touched in a dark moment, and from that time I've known health and life" (*The Way*, p. 262). He refers to the well-known story of his astonishing healing. Working desperately hard as a missionary evangelist, he lived with tensions and frustrations, trying to work, then failing to keep going. Once he broke down while preaching in the Philippines. One day, kneeling in the back of the Central Methodist Church in Lucknow, India, while praying for others, the Lord spoke to Brother Stanley: "Are you yourself ready for the work to which I have called you?" His honest reply was, "No, Lord, I'm done for. I've reached the end of my resources and I can't go on." The Spirit spoke again: "If you'll turn that problem over to me and not worry about it, I'll take care of it." Eagerly Jones replied, "Lord, I close the bargain right here." Dr. Jones testifies: "I arose from my knees knowing I was a well man.... I scarcely touched the earth as I walked along. I was possessed with life and health and peace. For days after that I wondered why I should ever go to bed" (*A Song of Ascents: A Spiritual Autobiography* [Nashville: Abingdon Press, 1968], p. 89). Today in that Lucknow church hangs a plaque that reads: "Here Dr. E. Stanley Jones, world evangelist, surrendered his physically shattered life to Christ and rose a whole man."

Dr. Jones went on to live long and vigorously, ministering both in India and in the rest of the world.

THROUGH THE RESURRECTION

Not everyone experiences healing as Dr. Jones did. Paul had a thorn in the flesh (2 Corinthians 12:7-11). Paul believed God did not heal him, even though he prayed three times, to keep him from being proud of his special revelations. Paul turned his focus away from the handicap onto God's call, and the hang-up became his gift.

Paul believed in life eternal and records what will happen to believers in the Resurrection (1 Corinthians 15). This Dr. Jones calls "the final cure" (*The Way*, p. 263). And cure it is! No more sorrow, no pain, no death; only peace, love, and beauty. The anticipation of us all—ill or well, in poverty or in wealth, in frustration or at peace—this lively hope motivates us to follow Jesus, Author of eternal life.

QUESTIONS

1. Do you see medicine as a gift of God? Does it help us become whole persons? Why do some people resist going to the doctor? Why do others insist on having more surgeries than necessary?
2. How does the psychosomatic principle relate to one's spirituality? Do you believe our spirits, emotions, and bodies interrelate?
3. Have you yourself experienced healing? Immediate healing? Process healing? Do you have some hints as to why God often heals over a period of time, and not always immediately?
4. What do you believe about life after death? How does the knowledge of life eternal relate to quality living here on earth?
5. What role do you see forgiveness playing in healing? Virginia Todd Holeman's definition of forgiveness will help you come to grips with this crucial issue: "The process of replacing negative emotions such as anger, rage, resentment and bitterness with positive emotions

such as empathy, compassion, humility and love." Dr. Holeman adds: "For members of God's reconciled kingdom, gratitude for our own forgiveness can motivate our desire to forgive one another" (*Reconcilable Differences*, p. 237).

V. WHERE DOES POWER IN PREACHING COME FROM?

Jesus is the gospel—he himself is the good news. (Christ of the Indian Road)

Stanley Jones saw the act of preaching as a profoundly Christ-centered experience, empowered by the Spirit of God. Yes, the preacher must prepare and prepare with care; Jones spent summer weeks annually in the mountains of India, preparing the messages he would deliver around the world in the next set of evangelistic meetings. Definitely, the preacher must be a diligent student of the Bible and apply truth in light of keen observation of life. All that and more constitute the human side of preaching; but truly incarnational preaching means God himself must invade and inspire, inbreathe and guide, the act of preaching.

Dr. Jones never failed to remind himself of the divine dimension of gospel preaching. Before every sermon, he requested the audience to sit in silence; while they prayed and opened their hearts to God's Word, Brother Stanley repeated to himself his life verse, John 15:16: "Ye have not chosen me, but I have chosen you, and ordained you, that ye should go and bring forth fruit, and that your fruit should remain: that whatsoever ye shall ask of the Father in my name, he may give it you" (KJV). This ritual of silence, which Stanley Jones never skipped, reminded him that God himself had called him to preach and that fruit comes from the Father in the name of Jesus.

God incarnates the sermon through Jesus and the gospel. What, precisely, is that gospel? It is to that foundational question we now turn.

THE GOSPEL WE PREACH

"There are four pillars upon which Christ's gospel rests: his Life, his Cross, his Resurrection, and his Coming into the lives of men—Pentecost" (*Christ of Every Road: A Study in Pentecost* [London: Hodder and Stoughton, 1930], p. 68). Today, scholars would call the four pillars a kind of mini-*kerygma* (the proclaimed gospel). Jones published *The Christ of Every Road* in 1930, six years before C. H. Dodd's seminal *The Apostolic Preaching and Its Developments* (Grand Rapids: Baker Book House, 1936). Professor Dodd, the well-known British New Testament scholar, itemized the components of *kerygma*, the gospel preached by the New Testament apostles. Before Dodd's book we did not talk much about the *kerygma*. Since Dodd, authorities such as the careful scholar Robert Mounce have studied *kerygma* in still greater detail, enriching our knowledge of the content and implications of the gospel. Jones stands ahead of his time, seeing clearly what some did not see so vividly, in delineating the gospel that brings salvation.

Dr. Mounce found, by analytical study of the New Testament, that the *kerygma* falls into nine components in three parts:

> *The proclamation of the*
> 1. Death,
> 2. Resurrection, and
> 3. Exaltation of our Lord
> 4. All seen as the fulfillment of prophecy and
> 5. Involving man's responsibility.
>
> *The resultant evaluation of Jesus as both*
> 6. Lord and
> 7. Christ.
>
> *On this basis hearers of the gospel must*
> 8. Repent and
> 9. Receive forgiveness.

(Robert H. Mounce, *The Essential Nature of New Testament Preaching* [Grand Rapids: Eerdmans, 1960], p. 77)

Note that the *kerygma* relates entirely to Jesus Christ; each of the nine components makes sense only as they relate to him. Christ and his message constitute Christianity; he brings wholeness and salvation. That central fact the Christian preacher always keeps in view; indeed, he or she can never quit talking about Jesus and the need for repentance and forgiveness, along with other implications of the good news. Just there—in Jesus and his good news—lies the primary power in preaching.

The life, death, and resurrection of Jesus—the first three pillars of Dr. Jones's mini-*kerygma*—remind us of Paul: "While Jews clamor for miraculous demonstrations and Greeks go in for philosophical wisdom, we go right on proclaiming Christ, the Crucified. Jews treat this like an *anti*-miracle—and Greeks pass it off as absurd. But to us who are personally called by God himself—both Jews and Greeks—Christ is God's ultimate miracle and wisdom all wrapped up in one" (1 Corinthians 1:22-24 *Message*).

Paul sees the cross and resurrection of our Lord as absolutely fundamental. In 1 Corinthians 15, he writes about the Resurrection in some detail. He never tires of preaching Christ crucified, resurrected, and alive in the hearts of his people. All this Paul and other New Testament writers relate to Old Testament prophesies of the Messiah. They never quit celebrating his life and works—the power content in preaching.

The lordship of Christ, made real to thousands after Peter's sermon at Pentecost (Acts 2), finds transformational expression in our Lord's disciples, documented in Acts. Each of Mounce's nine components, articulated in the sermons of the early church, realize fulfillment in the lives of first-century Christians. We locate the specific elements of the preached gospel, the *kerygma*, by isolating the common denominators in those earliest proclamations.

What we preach—the gospel—gripped New Testament proclaimers completely and motivated them to call for evangelistic decision. But what about the proclaimer himself or herself?

THE PREACHER

Stanley Jones confronts preachers head-on: "Unconverted or half-converted ministers in the pulpit produce unconverted or half-converted people" (*Conversion* [New York: Abingdon Press, 1959], p. 28). In other words, repentance and forgiveness cannot be halfway measures.

Just here, in conversion, lies motivation for sharing the gospel.

> After fifty-six years I still want to put my arms around the world and share this with everybody. That is the reason I can't retire. I hope my dying gasp will be the words of Wesley: "I commend my Savior to you." If and when I get to heaven I expect to ask for forty-eight hours of rest. . . . Then I'll ask for twenty-four hours to look around heaven and meet my friends. Then I'll go up to Jesus and say: " . . . haven't you a fallen world somewhere where they need an evangelist of the good news? Please send me." (*Conversion*, p. 39)

Authentic motivation for gospel preaching finds its initial source in conversion to Christ. But there's more.

THE ROLE OF THE SPIRIT IN PREACHING

Conversion introduces the conscious mind to a fresh sense of cleanness and new loyalty. So real, fulfilling, and motivating is this new life in Christ that one thinks the inner battle with self has come to an end. But the honeymoon days stop within the first year of the new life. Subconscious urges "stunned into insensibility by the introduction of this new and different and authoritative life in the conscious mind, now . . . reassert themselves." Angers, fears, moodiness, resentments—all supposed gone—now rear their ugly heads from "the storm cellars of the subconscious." Conscious and subconscious minds go to war (*Conversion*, p. 229).

Many Christians, even preachers, settle for a pre-Pentecost life, believing the war must continue. But can one even remotely imagine the apostles after Acts 2 preaching with an uncertain sound, fumbling about, hesitant, inadequate, and defeated? Nor can cleverness explain the astonishing power of these men—plain, ordinary folk doing extraordinary things. Notice their thought, lifestyle, stability and balance, and their sustained enthusiasm even when thrown into prison. Only Pentecost can explain these men, some unschooled, who "turned the world upside down" (Acts 17:6 RSV).

That dynamic—the Holy Spirit—available to God's called ministers, explains not only the spread of the gospel in the early church, but also the sense of urgency and the accompanying fulfillment that characterizes authoritative preachers throughout history.

Brother Stanley writes at length about Spirit-empowered living. He spells out the steps into the experience and maintenance of life in God in *Abundant Living* (New York: Abingdon Press 1942, pp. 156–58). In nearly everything Dr. Jones publishes or preaches, he comes to grips with Spirit-empowered life and ministry.

EFFECTIVE PREACHING MODELED

The spiritual component in effective preachers takes primacy, but what about the human part of this incarnational business called preaching? Even as Jesus was fully God and fully human, so preaching must be both divine and human.

I sat on a campus bench with Stanley Jones in Seattle, Washington, sharing with him that I would soon leave my present job as college professor to teach preaching at Asbury Theological Seminary. I asked for counsel. His one-sentence answer I cannot forget: "Preaching is caught more than taught."

This by no means undermines the classroom; education takes its time-tested place in the preparation of clergy. One cannot listen to Dr. Jones's sermons on tape or read his writings without awareness of his grasp of rhetoric, logic, and communication theory. He saw clearly the need for preachers-in-the-making to study diligently, and also to hear good preaching themselves. Hearing it over and over again, and from masters, creates contagion for effective pulpit communication. (Suggestion: subscribe to *Preaching Today*, the monthly audio series, which includes two powerful sermons with each mailing, along with full manuscripts. Each CD also includes an interview on the art of preaching or a workshop by a homiletics professor. Call 800-806-7796 or go online at www.ChristianityToday.com/go/pta/).

Dr. Jones was a master pulpit communicator. "Stanley Jones has always been a preacher's preacher" (Eunice Jones Mathews and James K. Mathews, compilers, *Selections from E. Stanley Jones: Christ and Human Need* [Nashville: Abingdon Press, 1972], p. 13). To reveal the reason he was a preacher's preacher uncovers secrets of his contagious public communication.

SECRETS OF CONTAGION

"Interest grows on information," goes the time-honored adage. Exciting preachers find data to enhance understanding and illumination of the gospel. The Mathews say that Brother Stanley "has been an acute observer of the human scene, of literature and life, alert for anything which would shed light on man's experience of the gospel" (*Selections*, p. 13).

The exciting gospel communicator never tires of gathering data for preaching. Principles used in the acquisition and communication of knowledge reveal secrets of pulpit power:

(1) *Listening.* Whether listening to a Hindu, an atheist, a doctor, or an engineer, to a farmer or shoe salesman—to anyone—Jones took in facts. His mind soaked up information like a sponge absorbs water.

Contagious preachers listen eagerly for information. (Suggestion: Explore the literature on listening. For example, Chalice Press publishes a whole series of books on listening. Go to www.chalicepress.com, call 800-366-3383, or e-mail customerservice@cbp21.com. See also *Hearing Beyond the Words: How to Become a Listening Pastor* by Emma J. Justes [Nashville: Abingdon Press, 2006]. This is available through Cokesbury bookstores, 800-672-1789, or www.cokesbury.com.)

(2) *Focus*. In an unpublished manuscript, Jones records how he writes a book. A project takes two years, the first year for data gathering. In that year, his mind acts as a magnet, drawing material on the specific theme he will develop. He used a similar principle for sermon making.

Stimulating preachers search for illuminating material focused on specific preaching texts.

(3) *Looking*. Jesus quoted an old Jewish proverb about people who have eyes to see but do not perceive, and ears to hear but do not understand (Matthew 13:14). Insightful preachers see past the obvious, resulting in fresh interpretations of scripture and life.

One listens to that kind of preaching and says, *Those facts had escaped me, but now I see!*

(4) *Honesty*. Jones revealed what he saw and heard. He refused to varnish facts to make himself or others look good.

When we're authentic—lacking in artifice—preaching becomes real and therefore inviting. Duplicity turns people off; sincerity creates a listening atmosphere.

(5) *Application*. Facts in themselves do not create contagion; but using and interpreting them to meet genuine need opens listeners' ears and triggers wills.

Appealing preachers show how gospel truth meets specific human needs, much like a well-tailored suit fits with precision.

(6) *Mastery*. Command of facts gives authority to preachers. Conscientious writing of sermons, word for word, aids memory and helps the minister do accurate preaching, or "scrapes the fungus from thought," as one of my preacher friends observes.

Mastering means confidence, releasing the preacher to freedom in delivery.

(7) *Mustness*. Dr. Jones sat in my Volkswagen bug on our way from the church, where he had just preached on healing, to his hotel. I asked the secret of his power in public address. He stuttered, seeming not to know of his pulpit contagion. Finally at the

front door of the hotel, his right foot on the curb, Brother Stanley turned and said, "I must preach Christ." Sounds like John Wesley as he rode into Arbroath, Scotland, and cried, "I came to bring them Christ."

The chief fact in preaching is Christ, the all-powerful Change Agent. He changes lives radically, and that leads us to the application of the gospel.

THE DIDACHE

The adage "Interest grows on information" stands stalwart in the public speech arena, pulpit communication included. But the Christian communicator asks, "To what purpose?" Information for information's sake, though interesting and useful, does not do the job of life change. Only Christ does that.

Scripture tells us that Jesus is "the way, and the truth, and the life" (John 14:6 RSV). The Spirit of truth leads us into all truth. Truth translates into loving acts, the fruit of the Spirit (John 15:16-17). Jesus taught people how to put feet to truth. How can we, by our teaching and preaching, help people do just that? The answer lies in what scholars call *didache*, the teaching part of the preaching task.

Kerygma and *didache* belong together. The one, the gospel that saves, brings people to Christian conversion. *Didache* explains in detail the ethical implications of the gospel that saves. *Kerygma* is the foundation of the ethical application of the gospel.

Picture a house. The foundation is *kerygma*, the superstructure *didache*. To put up the superstructure of justice, social reform, and personal behavior on sand means collapse in the storms of life. But to construct the house of application and ethics on the solid foundation of gospel substance means the building will hold in stormy weather.

The preacher's task, then, is twofold: to win converts and to nurture them in gospel living. To preach the Word, with its vivid pictures of sin and judgment and its equally vivid painting of sin's cure in Christ, his cross, and Resurrection—that's the solid declaration God uses to save his children. To go further, to teach (*didache* means "to teach") converts how to live out the gospel in home, workplace, and community, that's where the rubber hits the road, the proof the gospel works.

Just as Paul uses the first part of his epistles for making doctrine clear, then makes applications at the end of his letters, so the preacher lays the kerygmatic foundation on which he or she builds to show implications for the practice of Christianity.

Taking repentance is one element of the *kerygma*. The didactic implications of repentance include the fruits of the spirit: love, joy, peace, patience, kindness, goodness, faithfulness, gentleness, self-control (Galatians 5:22-23). Just before listing the fruits of the Spirit, Paul itemizes the works of the flesh: immorality, impurity, licentiousness, idolatry, sorcery, enmity, strife, jealousy, anger, selfishness, dissension, party spirit, envy, drunkenness, carousing (vv. 19-21). Paul, in these verses, writes to Christians who have repented of their sins and received forgiveness from Christ. They have heard the gospel and believed; yet they must grow to maturity because they still struggle with the old lifestyle. Paul makes specific the contrast between the pre-converted life and the expectations of the converted life, thus nurturing the Galatian Christians toward spiritual adulthood.

To preach both *kerygma* and *didache*, to keep them in balance—that is what the Christian preacher must do. To overemphasize one creates unbalanced Christians. To preach both results in healing and wholeness, illumination and understanding, knowledge and practice. But to spend an inordinate amount of pulpit time on the kerygmatic side, emphasizing conversion but minimizing nurture, results in undeveloped and immature disciples. By the same token, to invest too much time on the didactic side creates Christians who may know about morality but know little about its underpinnings and power to implement Christian living.

This balanced proclamation scholars call *didactic-kerygma*, and their studies reveal that the New Testament never really segregates the saving gospel and its nurturing components. The two go together; they belong together. So when we announce the gospel in any of its parts, we must always show something of its implications in daily living. Conversely, when we preach some aspect of the practice of Christianity, we must remind our people of the theological foundation that provides the dynamic for living out the gospel.

Now we must tackle the how of preaching the gospel with its applications.

PICTURE PREACHING

"People do picture thinking" goes the proverb. Abstractions leave listeners cold; pictures create lively response. Try to find a page in Stanley Jones's books without a picture—seldom if ever possible. Try to find a chapter in Holy Scripture without a picture; even the arguments of Paul use plenty of them.

Our picture-oriented culture—TV, magazines, oversized illustration books, computer screens, cell phones that take pictures, photostreaming—calls for *vivid* communication. Some pastors use movie clips to help them preach. Worship leaders put words with nature scenes on screens to assist the audience in sung praise.

With this radical change in our culture, theologians began in recent decades to write about narrative (story) theology. Then the homileticians caught on, and now narrative (picture) preaching is the in thing. It takes many expressions and requires the discipline of responsible Bible interpretation. (See Thomas Long's helpful analysis and defense of narrative preaching, "What Happened to Narrative Preaching?" *Journal for Preachers* 28, no. 4 [Pentecost 2005]: pp. 9–14.)

What, then, are the techniques for doing picture preaching, the vehicle of gospel communication for our time?

Tell stories. George, a thirteen-year alcoholic, had tried thirteen cures. Thoroughly discouraged, he determined to take his life but did not want authorities to find his body in a dirty suit. The check-out lady at a Salvation Army thrift store, though unaware of his plan for self-destruction, but perhaps sensing the deep need of the man, invited him to the evening worship service in the chapel. People would be gathering in a few minutes. George reasoned that he could wait to commit suicide. He listened to the gospel; God revealed himself to the destitute man; George's life underwent radical change—conversion from sin and disease to Christ and wholeness.

Time passed, and George heard God's call to preach the gospel that saved him. When I had him in preaching class, he had completed thirteen years in Christian ministry. I call him the 13-13-13 man.

Such a story! A true story. It paints a picture and could serve as the beginning of a sermon entitled "You Must Be Born Again" (John 3:16).

Tell stories that translate the Bible for people today. Currently published versions of the Scriptures—for example, the New Living Translation and Eugene Peterson's *The Message*—help. These two versions especially relate to the picture-oriented character of our culture and in turn suggest illustrations from your own experience and observation.

The story of George plugs into our alcoholic culture and into the enormous receptiveness we now enjoy for supernatural change.

Tell stories that exegete the Bible for what it actually says. Exegesis means getting *out of* Scripture what is truly there; *eisegesis* means reading *into* Scripture what the preacher or someone else wants to see there. True, many Bible passages contain not one truth but facets of truths. But deliberately, even unknowingly, to interpret a section of Scripture to make it say something not intended leads people astray.

The picture above of the 13-13-13 man rightly exegetes "you must be born again." The John 3 passage calls for life change; George experienced life change.

The challenge lies in discerning just what a passage means, which is not always easy, because the Bible, couched in a different time and culture, calls for digging into customs, language, and ancient thought forms. To help us do that, we have a rich supply of commentaries, Bible dictionaries, and custom books available.

And those kinds of reference tools continue to come off the presses, thus reflecting current scholarship and updating our understanding of Scripture.

PREACHER FORMATION

It takes time to grow a soul. Preacher Billy Graham bemoans his too-busy life. He could have spent less time on the road, and more time "growing my soul," he declares. Mr. Graham speaks for us all because preacher formation takes time—time in prayer, meditation, study, and living.

The three ways we communicate undergo maturation, and sometimes radical change, as we grow up into Christ. The three are language, tone, and body language.

Language. Words or semantics stand as important vehicles of communication. Time with the Word not only shows us what God wants to reveal to preacher and people, but also eventually reveals that words are powerful, rather like stones thrown into a pond, the ripples spreading in ever-increasing breadth and distance. The Bible sees words as *acts*.

Once the great fact of the Word and its potential lays hold of the preacher's soul, the preacher handles Scripture and its interpretation with both care and excitement. What might words do in the heart of a listener? Eugene Peterson's translation of Proverbs 25:11-12 exposes the power of words:

> The right word at the right time
> > is like a custom-made piece of jewelry,
> And a wise friend's timely reprimand
> > is like a gold ring slipped on your finger. (*Message*)

Part of the maturation process relates to the sometimes difficult business of grammar and syntax. The more accurately and the more carefully we use our tongue, the sharper, the more penetrating, the spoken word.

Tone. Technically known as tonetics or tonality, the more pleasant and persuasive one's vocal projections, the more the preacher gets through to the listeners. (Suggestion: If you sense sandpaper in your voice, consult a competent speech teacher or laryngologist.)

Once the Spirit of God captivates the whole preacher, he or she takes on neither an artificial holy tone, nor a kind of purple prose, but the spirit of glad invitation.

As you mature vocally, you discover your own voice and—miracle of miracles—God speaks through it! He does, and in a way he speaks through no other voice.

Body language. We call this kinesics, a term that comes from the Greek word for "motion." Interestingly, well over half the total communication process relates to kinesics. If the preacher speaks with poise, not flailing the air or pacing, something of the dignity and profound relevance of God and life and the gospel come through to people. How one dresses, the magic of gestures matching the spoken word—all combine to make or break public address.

For the spiritually discerning, soul-growing preacher, each of the three vehicles of communication develops with study, prayer, meditation, and connection with God's people. The very struggle of developing oneself into a preacher has the touch of God's hand on it. More, the preacher formation process carries potential for creating art marked by the power that calls people to Christ and to his gospel.

SUMMARY: SOURCES OF POWER

Sources of preaching power include the following:

> *Jesus Himself*—He *is* Christianity, the Redeemer, the Life Changer.
>
> *The Gospel*—Good news about Jesus, his life, and his ministry. Get firmly in mind the *kerygma*, what we preach.
>
> *Scripture*—The written Word made real by the Spirit brings Life.

A *divine call to preach*—Study John 15:16 in the light of your own call.

Conversion—God has a hard time using half-converted people.

The Spirit—He brings Life through personal Pentecost.

Models of good preaching—To catch the work of the pulpit in its wholeness and its nuances creates preacher perception that develops into effective proclamation.

Contagion—Enthusiasm marked by authenticity relates naturally to hungry hearts.

Didache—People want to know how to apply the gospel, for everyone knows intuitively that living in the Spirit of Jesus is proof of the pudding.

Story—Narrative preaching translates abstractions into understandable pictures.

Formation—Our people want to see a growing expositor; stale preachers feed souls sparsely.

Words, tone, and body language—Parishioners expect their preacher to care about them; one of the best ways to let them know they are cared for is to prepare carefully. How do I craft with words? Does my tone project concern? Does body language reflect dignity?

QUESTIONS

1. At this stage in your journey toward becoming a preacher, how do you see yourself developing into an authentic preacher? What growth instruments will you use to take advantage of your growing edges? (You may want to see "Growth Sheets" at the close of Donald E. Demaray's *Introduction to Homiletics*, 3rd ed. [Indianapolis: Light and Life Communications, 2006]).

2. Would you like to enhance your understanding of key terms such as *homily, homiletics,* and *hermeneutics?* See William H. Willimon and Richard Lischer, *Concise Encyclopedia of Preaching* (Louisville, Ky.: Westminster John Knox Press, 1995).
3. What preachers serve as models for you? Why?
4. List offending elements: overdressing, screaming, exaggeration in both storytelling and body language, and so on. Why do these pulpit behaviors turn people off? Do you see theological/spiritual as well as psychological and cultural answers?
5. Why do we see Jesus as the ideal preacher?

VI. JOY IN THIS WORLD?

The deepest joy is the communion of Person with person. Sometimes our earthly vessels can scarecely contain the weight of this exquisite joy. We are almost tempted to ask Him to stay His hand. But we wouldn't have Him do it for worlds, for this is Life, Life. (Victorious Living)

My friend Ajith Fernando, passionate gospel worker and social reformer, organized teams to help restore Sri Lanka's devastated areas and homeless people after the historic tsunami of late 2004. This was quite a challenge in a country that forbids evangelization, and whose governmental authorities threaten new Christians with jail. "How do we fulfill the Great Commission?" Ajith asks. "Please pray for us in Sri Lanka."

But listen to what he writes next:

> Nothing, however, can dampen our joy in the Lord. I simply can't get over the fact that eternal God has saved us and continues to love us in spite of our numerous failures. This is what gives [us] the strength for suffering and service and what keeps us happy amidst threats and fears. More and more I am coming to recognize what a wonderful gift God's joy is. Recently I have been meditating on a song I learned in Sunday school.

> > Joy, joy, joy; with joy my heart is ringing.
> > Joy, joy, joy; His love to me is known.
> > My sins are all forgiven; I'm on my way to
> >   heaven.
> > My heart is bubbling over with this joy, joy, joy.

> So simple, and yet so true! May God energize you with His joy. (Letter dated April 2005)

JOY IN A WORLD GONE MAD?

What never ceases to amaze even the casual reader of the Bible is the recurrence of *joy*. Look in your Bible concordance for words such as *joy*, *joyous*, and *joyful*, and find many references and columns of verses. Yet Scripture paints a bleak picture of the world: war, sickness, reverses—all the human experiences that one would expect to rob people of contentment.

What could possibly explain this incredible joy? George McDonald gets at the answer when he declares, "It is the heart that is not yet sure of its God that is afraid to laugh in his presence" (*Sir Gibbie* [Whitehorn, Calif.: Johannesen, 1992], p. 155). Right on! Read the Psalms and repeatedly find the psalmist declaring himself absolutely sure of his God; this deep security breeds joy (Psalms 4:7, 47:1, 98, and so on). Joy in spite of threat and persecution!

Or observe the early Christians—beaten, thrown into jail, verbally abused, yet full of joy. At the outset of Acts 8 we're told "a great persecution arose against the church in Jerusalem" (v. 1 RSV). Did this deter the early followers of Jesus? Not in the least. They mustered their forces and performed miracles, whereupon we read, "So there was much joy in that city" (v. 8 RSV). Or look in Acts 13 in which we read of freshly initiated persecution; yet the chapter concludes, "And the disciples were filled with joy and with the Holy Spirit" (v. 52 RSV). "The blood of the martyrs is the seed of the Church," observed Tertullian.

Joy characterizes saints right through the centuries. Franco Zeffirelli's St. Francis film, *Brother Sun, Sister Moon*, exposes the great joy that helps us define St. Francis. Mother Teresa worked daily with the poorest of the poor, but can you imagine her a sad person? Sing the hymns of St. Bernard of Clairvaux; can such joy come from an ascetic?

Surely one of the historic requirements in the canonization process for sainthood is joy.

ST. FRANCIS'S SECRET

Saint Francis of Assisi tells in his *Little Flowers* of teaching Brother Leo about real joy. He relates an imaginary story. Walking in the cold and snow, he finds a house and knocks, hoping to secure shelter. Turned away, he knocks at the same house again only to suffer rejection again, and then again.

> Yet, for Christ's love
> we behave with patience and cheer,
> focusing on Jesus' sufferings;
>> Oh! Brother Leo,
>> this is real joy!"
> (Donald E. Demaray, *Little Flowers of St. Francis* [New York: Alba House, 1992], p. 35)

Saint Francis informed Brother Leo that healing people of blindness, exorcising demons, and acquiring vast amounts of knowledge do not produce joy. But victory over self—ah!—that brings joy.

> So, Brother Leo, the conclusion is this:
>> The Spirit's best gift,
>> His highest grace,
>>> Christ gives to His friends:
>>> *To conquer self*
>>> For Jesus' sake. (ibid.)

A GIVING SPIRIT

Everyone delights in giving. My dad, in his sunset years, gave me so many things I felt embarrassed. My sister Margaret's keen insight helped me: "Mother's gone and dad needs someone to give to." Evidently God has built into us the need to give. Part of the *imago dei* (the Latin term for "created in the image of God") is the need to give. And who doesn't find reward and real joy in giving?

If, however, one gives in order to get something in return, both giver and receiver get hurt. Sincere giving comes from genuine love, and the reward of true affection is sweet fruit.

This explains the reason the saints and the mystics talked about giving in radical terms. Jesus did too. The one who gives self finds self; the one who does not, never quite defines himself or herself. Eugene Peterson's translation of Matthew 10:39 makes vivid the principle of self-giving: "If your first concern is to look after yourself, you'll never find yourself. But if you forget about yourself and look to me, you'll find both yourself and me" (*Message*).

Self-giving often means suffering. But why does suffering relate to joy?

SUFFERING AND JOY

Really now, suffering relates to joy? Put the question personally: Why must I carry the cross of self-giving?

When we live like Christ, self-discovery emerges—suffering peels away artifice, much like cutting away the outer skin of an onion. When the unusable disappears, the usable appears; when the inauthentic goes, the authentic emerges. There is no joy like discovering and being one's true self. And that is precisely what leads to unencumbered and productive service.

Listen to Paul's declaration from prison: "I am glad when I suffer for you in my body, for I am completing what remains of Christ's sufferings for his body, the church" (Colossians 1:24 NLT). Eugene Peterson helps us see Paul's remarkable declaration in full context: "I want you to know how glad I am that it's me sitting here in this jail and not you. There's a lot of suffering to be entered into in this world—the kind of suffering Christ takes on. I welcome the chance to take my share in the church's part of that suffering. When I became a servant in this church, I experienced this suffering as a sheer gift, God's way of helping me serve you, laying out the whole truth" (Colossians 1:24-25 Message).

No self-pity there! A twentieth-century mystic and social worker said we must look for self-pity like we look for lice. Death to self brings authenticity, freedom, and joy, the joy that characterized the earliest Christians—resurrection Christians.

THE RESURRECTION CONNECTION

"Each morning at the close of our morning prayers at our Ashram the leader says, 'The Lord is risen!' and the group answers, 'He is risen indeed.' In that strength we go forward into the day knowing the power of His resurrection" (*Victorious Living* [New York: Abingdon-Cokesbury Press, 1936], p. 313). Yes! Authentic Christians really believe in Jesus and in his life, death, and Resurrection; they live joyously, and they laugh and live life to the full.

Early on in the history of the Eastern Orthodox Church, a most interesting custom developed. The day following Easter Sunday, clergy and people went to church to tell jokes. The reason? To laugh at the devil! He only *thought* he had put Jesus to death. God played an enormous trick on Satan: Jesus rose from the dead! He's alive!

The fact that the Resurrection kept the early Christians going despite persecution not only explains the existence and spread of the Church, but also filled Jesus' followers with genuine hope. Hope creates joy. Paul wrote, "May the God of hope fill you with all joy and peace in believing, so that you may abound in hope by the power of the Holy Spirit" (Romans 15:13). (For more scripture on the relation of hope and joy, see, for example, Hebrews 12:2, Isaiah 55:12, and Romans 5:2.)

Combine hope with the living presence of Christ in these early Christians, and they simply could not exist other than joyously. That spirit, along with the Orthodox Church's Monday-after-Easter custom, has entered Protestant churches. Some churches celebrate on the Sunday after Easter with joyous and humorous stories, balloons, and anything at all that communicates the grand delight of believing Christians.

Saint Augustine called true followers of the resurrected Lord "Hallelujah Christians."

THE CHURCH AND JOY

If Jesus did not rise from the dead, how do we explain the existence and expansion of the church? The resurrection of our Lord proved beyond a shadow of a doubt that he is indeed the Savior. Christians really are redeemed! Christians have a future! Christians realize fulfillment! Christians anticipate, with exhilarating vigor, the heaven to come!

If the empty tomb were not reality, the church, with its excitement about this life and the next, could not possibly have come into being. The genius of Jesus, with his amazing insight and wisdom, might have given rise to a short-term organization, but that grand sense of the "called out" (*ecclesia*, the New Testament word for "church," means "the called-out ones") from the world, with its stinging and debilitating pessimism, could not have lasted long.

As a child, I loved going to church. Only in adulthood did I have enough perspective to learn why. My Sunday school and junior church leaders came across consistently as happy people. They did not have to make an announcement (*Look! I'm a happy Christian*); one only needed to see their glad faces, listen to their cheerful voices, and hear the hope in their stories.

They laughed easily. They lived by the classic mirth passages of the Old Testament: "A cheerful heart is a good medicine, / but a downcast spirit dries up the bones" (Proverbs 17:22); "Anxiety weighs down the human heart, / but a good word cheers it up" (Proverbs 12:25); "A cheerful heart has a continual feast" (Proverbs 15:15b). We heard the New Testament verses on joy: "Rejoice in the Lord always; again I will say, Rejoice" (Philippians 4:4); "That my joy may be in you, and that your joy may be complete" (John 15:11); "I came that they may have life, and have it abundantly" (John 10:10b). (Quotations in this paragraph are from NRSV.)

Laughter, joy, and humor characterize normal Christians. This explains the great seventeenth-century theologian Richard Baxter's wise instruction: "Keep company with the more cheerful sort of the godly; there is no mirth like the mirth of believers." Stanley Jones sometimes ended his Ashrams (retreats) with a humor evening—sketches, skits, stories, readings—anything at all to bring a smile to lips and a laugh from hearts. I have watched him embrace mirth with his whole being, expressing the joy that never failed to characterize him even in times of crisis and personal loss. One very funny Stanley Jones story relates to a little urchin boy, stark naked, in India. Asked his name, the little boy replied, "E. Stanley Jones." As in other cultures, Indian society loves to name children after famous people.

Churchgoing people are characterized by joy. James S. Stewart, the contagious Scottish preacher, declared, "When Christian worship is dull and joyless, Jesus Christ has been left outside—that is the only possible explanation." Isaiah says God promises that he will make his faithful followers "joyful in my house of prayer" (Isaiah 56:7). Paul sees the true source of joy not in wine but in God's Spirit: "Don't drink too much wine. That cheapens your life. Drink the Spirit of God, huge draughts of him. Sing hymns instead of drinking songs! Sing songs from your heart to Christ. Sing praises over everything, any excuse for a song to God the Father in the name of our Master, Jesus Christ" (Ephesians 5:18-20 *Message*).

THE JOY OF ANTICIPATION: HEAVEN

Larry King recently interviewed Billy Graham for the twenty-fourth time. Larry thought Billy held the record for the most number of interviews on *Larry King Live*. At the outset of the interview, Larry asked Dr. Graham about his health. Dr. Graham had suffered a broken hip and wrestled with other physical challenges, but his chief ongoing problem is hydrocephalus—in lay terms, water on the brain. He has gone through four surgeries to drain the excess fluid, and one time he thought he would die. He told the Lord of his readiness, even eagerness, to go to heaven. But parading before his mind's eye, in terrible succession, came his sins of the past. Not a happy picture until the Lord spoke: "Billy, my blood covers all your sins."

Peace enveloped Dr. Graham's soul; doubts fled and have stayed completely away in the intervening years.

Larry, in typical King style, asked if Billy suffered any hesitation about dying. "None whatsoever," came the quick and definitive answer. "Why?" Larry wanted to know. Billy answered that he had absolutely no doubt about heaven. In fact, he anticipates eagerly his arrival because, in heaven, no sin or evil of any kind can take up residence.

No viewer of that remarkable interview could have missed the joy and peace on Dr. Graham's face.

The Bible tells us precious little about eternal life, no doubt to keep us from being, as the old saying goes, "so heavenly minded that we're of no earthly good." The Bible does assure us of the fact of heaven, and that by the witness of our Lord himself: "You trust God, don't you? . . . There is plenty of room for you in my Father's home. If that weren't so, would I have told you that I'm on my way to get a room ready for you? And if I'm on my way to get your room ready, I'll come back and get you so you can live where I live" (John 14:1-4 *Message*).

Interestingly, whenever the Bible refers to heaven or the second coming, hope comes through loud and clear. For example, the Acts 1:6-11 paragraph, which ends with the promise of Christ's second coming, gives us such positive words as *Kingdom, witness, power, Holy Spirit,* and *heaven.* No fear there, only joy!

The old Methodists admonished their people to:

- Think about heaven
- Pray about heaven
- Sing about heaven
- Talk about heaven
- Preach about heaven
- Look forward to heaven

No wonder John Wesley observed, "Methodists die well." Anyone sure of heaven, such as Billy Graham and John Wesley, lives with the sheer joy of eager anticipation.

SOURCES AND RESOURCES OF JOY

(1) *Conversion.* You may want to read C. S. Lewis's spiritual autobiography, *Surprised by Joy.* Release from atheism and deism to belief in a personal God as embodied in Jesus Christ brought exhilarating surprise to C. S. Lewis.

Stanley Jones believed conversion must go deep enough to affect our reactions. Someone came to him after one of his sermons and said he found three things wrong with the address. Dr. Jones replied, "If you found only three things wrong you are better off than I am because I found seven things that I have to improve on in my sermon!" (E-mail from Stanley Jones' friend Sam Kamaleson, 15 June 2005).

(2) *The Holy Spirit, Author of joy.* As we grow in sanctification, we mature, becoming more and more like Jesus. Joy grows with ongoing spiritual formation. No wonder Luke says of the early Christians, "And the disciples were filled with joy and with the Holy Spirit" (Acts 13:52). Paul observed that the Thessalonian Christians "received the word with joy inspired by the Holy Spirit" (1 Thessalonians 1:6). Galatians 5:22 tells us the Holy Spirit produces joy, one of the fruits of the Christian.

(3) *Christ and his kingdom.* Stanley Jones believed Jesus and his kingdom stand stalwart, upright, and unshakable. To come to settled faith in him brings security that in turn creates joy. First Peter 1:8 documents this: "Although you have not seen him, you love him; and even though you do not see him now, you believe in him and rejoice with an indescribable and glorious joy."

(4) *Righteous living.* A pastor came to Dr. Jones with the astonishing announcement, "I do not agree with you because I am living in adultery and am enjoying it!" Jones responded, "Enjoy it while it lasts because it will not last long" (Kamaleson, ibid.).

(5) *The Creation.* Nature, for the Christian, brings immense joy. Listen to Eugene Peterson's translation of a single verse out of Psalm 96:

> Let Wilderness turn cartwheels,
> Animals, come dance,
> Put every tree of the forest in the choir.
> (v. 12 *Message*)

(6) *The sovereignty of God.* From the same Psalm and the same translator, hear the outset of verse 10: "Get out the message—GOD Rules!" To know that God, not fickle humanity, stands in charge of the world brings enormous release and therefore joy.

(7) *Suffering.* First Peter 4:12 and 13 reads, "Dear friends, don't be surprised at the fiery trials you are going through, as if something strange were happening to you. Instead be very glad—because these trials make you partners with Christ in his suffering, and afteward you will have the wonderful joy of sharing his glory when it is displayed to all the world" (NLT). Eugene Peterson's rendering of these verses gives us further clarification of the relation of suffering to joy: "Friends, when life gets really difficult, don't jump to the conclusion that God isn't on the job. Instead be glad that you are in the very thick of what Christ experienced. This is a spiritual refining process, with glory just around the corner" (*Message*).

(8) *Trust.* "In him our hearts rejoice, / for we trust in his holy name" (Psalm 33:21 NIV).

(9) *Divine protection.* "I think how much you have helped me; / I sing for joy in the shadow of your protecting wings" (Psalm 63:7 NLT).

(10) *Rescue.* In Habakkuk 3, the prophet has just rehearsed the awful things that can happen to God's people. "Even though the fig trees have no blossoms, and there are no grapes on the vine; even though the olive crop fails, and the fields lie empty and barren; even though the flocks die in the fields, and the cattle barns are empty, yet I will rejoice in the LORD! I will be joyful in the God of my salvation. The Sovereign LORD is my strength! He will

make me as surefooted as a deer and bring me safely over the mountains" (3:17-19 NLT).

(11) *Relief after crisis.* The New Living Translation of the last paragraph of Psalm 126 documents the experience of true believers:

> Restore our fortunes, LORD,
>> as streams renew the desert.
> Those who plant in tears
>> will harvest with shouts of joy.
> They weep as they go to plant their seed,
>> but they sing as they return with the harvest.
>
> (vv. 4–6)

The Message translation of this passage enriches the picture even more:

> And now, GOD, do it again—
>> bring rains to our drought-stricken lives
> So those who planted their crops in despair
>> will shout hurrahs at the harvest,
> So those who went off with heavy hearts
>> will come home laughing, with armloads of
>>> blessing.

(12) *Divine resource.* Eugene Peterson once more:

> Joyfully you'll pull up buckets of water
>> from the wells of salvation.
> And as you do it, you'll say
> "Give thanks to GOD.
> Call out his name.
>> Ask him anything!"
>
> (Isaiah 12:3-4 *Message*)

(13) *Hope.* "Oh! May the God of green hope fill you up with joy, fill you up with peace, so that your believing lives, filled with

the life-giving energy of the Holy Sprit, will brim over with hope!" (Romans 15:13 *Message*).

(14) *Worship.* Of those who come to God, he says, "I will bring to my holy mountain, / and make them joyful in my house of prayer ..." (Isaiah 56:7a). To worship with God's people, to sense the *koinonia* (fellowship) created by God's Spirit—such joy!

(15) *God's mercy.* "I am overcome with joy because of your unfailing love, / for you have seen my troubles, / and you care about the anguish of my soul" (Psalm 31:7 NLT). Eugene Peterson renders that verse like this: "I'm leaping and singing in the circle of your love; / you saw my pain, / you disarmed my tormentors, / You didn't leave me in their clutches / but gave me room to breathe" (*Message*).

(16) *Heaven.* Job received a revelation of eternal life when he announced joyously,

> If only my words were written in a book—
>   better yet, chiseled in stone!
> Still, I know that God lives—the One who gives me
>   back my life—
>   and eventually he'll take his stand on earth.
> And I'll see him—even though I get skinned alive!—
>   see God myself, with my very own eyes.
>   Oh, how I long for that day!
>   (Job 19:23-27 *Message*)

QUESTIONS

1. What sources and resources of joy can you add to the sixteen above? How about positive lifestyle? An affirming attitude? Family? What else?

2. Ancient Bible commentators, taking their cue from the Greeks, believed Christians ought to be more sober than joyous, more serious than humorous. Picture the two

Grecian actor masks, one with down-turned lips, the other with a smile. Do you believe the down-turned face reflects the Bible accurately?

3. Measure your joy level, perhaps against the list in "Sources and Resources" above, plus against your own additions. Where do you detect growing edges? What steps can you take to live more joyously?

4. Do you believe the joy of the Lord does in fact relate to our effectiveness as witnesses? Why?

5. How does your belief system, your theology, relate to happy, fulfilled living?

VII. But I Am Only a Christian-in-the-Making

I know better how to live now at eighty-eight than I did at eighteen or twenty-eight, even though I am still an uncompleted person. (The Divine Yes)

Sitting at a desk in the archive room, I forgot how cold the building was; and as the hours passed, I didn't notice that I had forgotten lunch, nor did I realize how stiff my body had gotten after sitting in one position for so long. The reason? I was working my way through boxes of black notebooks and folders, each crammed full of yellowed, lined pages that were crowded with handwritten notes, the personal journals Stanley Jones kept through the decades. Almost every day he recorded all kinds of things: ideas from a book, the gist of a conversation, an observation about a place, or reflections on a passage of scripture. What impressed me was not only the discipline that it took to maintain the practice over such a span of time, or the dizzying array of places he traveled, people he met, or books he read, amazing as those things are. What struck me most was that these black notebooks traced the development of his soul. Like the rings of a great old oak tree, they steadily recorded his growth through all kinds of conditions and circumstances.

As I replaced the last binder in its box, I recalled one of Brother Stanley's favorite descriptions of himself. He never claimed to be a Christian, only a "Christian-in-the-making" (*A Song of Ascents* [Nashville: Abingdon Press, 1968], p. 44). Of course, the yellowed pages don't disclose everything. There are plenty of questions I wish I could ask him about some of his experiences, especially the most challenging ones. Nevertheless, his notes are priceless.

I've thought a lot about the appeal of those pages. I think the reason that time seemed to stand still for me the day when I first read them is because those writings touched my longing to grow. Perhaps that is also the reason that, next to the Lord's Prayer, my favorite prayer in the New Testament is Paul's prayer for the growth of Christians at Ephesus:

> I pray that, according to the riches of his glory, he may grant that you may be strengthened in your inner being with power through his Spirit, and that Christ may dwell in your hearts through faith, as you are being rooted and grounded in love. I pray that you may have the power to comprehend, with all the saints, what is the breadth and length and height and depth, and to know the love of Christ that surpasses knowledge, so that you may be filled with all the fullness of God. (Ephesians 3:16-19)

Those words connect Paul's longing for the Christians of Ephesus with God's yearning for them to become deeper, more authentic persons. Imagine the implications.

THE CONVERSION OF OUR LOVE

The opening lines of Paul's great prayer remind us that the Father's love is the ground of our lives; his Spirit, our invisible supply of inner strength; his Son, a resident presence whom we trust. The communion of the Triune God is like a circle of love into which we've been welcomed, or, to use Paul's metaphor, the soil in which our transplanted lives take root and grow.

We are most ourselves when we are grounded in God's immense love because of the imprint of his image on us. Often we live in tension with this destiny because all our lives there have been a constant stream of messages that we are unlovable as we are. We have lived with the illusion that the only way we can really be acceptable or complete is by putting ourselves first and by trying to make life revolve around us. So, our driving intention is to find what makes us happy, cures our loneliness, gives us pleasure, might make us famous, can earn us reputation, or can bring us power. How could God ever get to this center, this innermost place in us, and convert our love? Brother Stanley liked to tell Peter's story because Peter so closely resembles us.

The day Peter steps out of his boat to follow Jesus is just the beginning. He remained focused on himself for a long time after that. Turn the pages and notice his selfishness, his desire to have his way, his ambition to rise higher than the other disciples, his "what's in it for me" attitude.

Then one day, near the end, Jesus says to Peter: "Peter, when you are converted, strengthen your brothers." Shortly after that, Jesus predicts that one in his band will betray him and that the others will abandon him. Peter objects, declaring stubbornly that he will certainly never do such a thing! Shortly, the authorities capture Jesus, and Peter retreats into the shadows. Warming by a charcoal fire in a circle of strangers, to save his own skin, Peter denies that he even knows Jesus . . . three times.

After the shattering events of the next few days, Peter returns to Galilee and to his fishing business. What future is there for a defeated disciple? He and the others fish all night and catch nothing. As they are returning to port in the early morning darkness, they hear a stranger on the shore call out for them to throw their nets on the other side of the boat. When they do, there is an overwhelming catch of fish. Peter recognizes that the figure on the shore is Jesus, alive! He plunges into the water and swims at top speed to the shore.

Moments later, he and the others are sitting quietly around the charcoal fire where Jesus has cooked fish for their breakfast. Some are talking softly when Jesus interrupts with words that pierce Peter's heart: "Peter, do you love me more than these?" Remember: Peter had said that though everyone else might abandon Jesus, he would never be guilty of such a thing. He had declared that he would always be loyal to his friend. Jesus asks him the question a second time. When he asks him the third time, Peter is crushed.

Peter starts weeping. He denied Jesus three times, and now Jesus is asking three times if Peter really loves him. In these sobering moments something in Peter shifts. Sorrow over his own sins and failures melt before Jesus' unimaginable love and forgiveness.

Then Jesus says: "Follow me, Peter." It is the same invitation that started Peter on his journey in the first place. This time Peter responds at a deeper level. From now on, he will follow from the heart. Of course, his humanness is very obvious. An old insecurity stirs and surfaces, as if by habit. "Turning his head, Peter noticed the disciple Jesus loved following right behind. When Peter noticed him, he asked Jesus, 'Master, what's going to happen to *him*?' Jesus said, 'If I want him to live until I come again, what's that to you? You—follow me'" (John 21:20-22 *Message*).

From this point, Peter was converted in his heart of hearts, in the place in his soul where he desired to love and be loved. The moment Jesus captured Peter's heart was the moment Peter was really set free. Now he could strengthen his brothers. Why? Because his love wasn't focused on what he could get out of it. He wasn't hooked into the disciple band in an unhealthy way because of his need to win approval, or to assert his fragile ego in order to be a "somebody." Now his heart belonged to Jesus. He was free to love the others because "he belonged to them in a secondary way for he belonged to Jesus in a primary way. His love was redeemed" (*Conversion* [Nashville: Abingdon Press, 1959], p. 72).

Jesus told Peter: "Feed my sheep." Over the years that followed, as Peter gave nourishment to others, he himself was fed and nourished. That seems to be a reliable principle: when we share God's love, our own lives are filled; but when we attempt to use others to scavenge some approval, attention, or affirmation for ourselves, we become even more famished. That's why Jesus could say to us: "I've told you these things for a purpose: that my joy might be your joy, and your joy wholly mature. This is my command: Love one another the way I loved you" (John 15:11-13 *Message*).

ROOTED AND GROUNDED IN LOVE

Rooted in love, we awaken each day with a mission: to show God's love and extend forgiveness to others every chance we have. As we do so, God uses our experiences to reveal even more to us about his love.

Paul prayed that the Ephesian Christians would "comprehend, with all the saints" (Ephesians 3:18) the unfathomable and mysterious power of God's love in every dimension of life. In other words, that together they would discover more about God's love than they could ever experience independently, apart from the companionship of the others.

Each of us thrives by giving and receiving love, and the actions of one person contribute to the lives of the rest. With God's love at the center, our lives are like tiny atoms with their nuclei. Atoms don't function independently, unrelated to surrounding atoms, but together they form a cell. Cells are not isolated, but make up tissue. Tissues make up organs, and all the organs together form a body. Health in the smallest part affects the well-being of the whole.

(1). *The breadth of God's love.* How liberating it is when we realize that God's love extends and applies to every part of our life. It was this paradigm shift that Stanley Jones experienced on board a ship bound for India to begin his work as a missionary. One day, somewhere on the Pacific Ocean, he reflected on the significance of the words the Inner Voice had spoken to him as a student at Asbury College. "It's India," said the voice; not "It's Indians." He explained: "India was to be the center of my endeavors, but Indians and non-Indians were my field. I would not be a professional missionary to Indians, but a personal missionary to everybody" (*A Song of Ascents*, p. 77). With such a perspective, he saw that he was in ministry wherever, and with whomever. That is an important discovery about the breadth of God's love.

Think of it: some people may think of you as a secretary, but that shows how little they know! You are God's agent anywhere, so long as you maintain his perspective on things. That change in your outlook touches people around you in the most surprising ways.

Here's another example. A pastor often prayed for God to remove his fear, but he still trembled with stage fright whenever he had to speak in public. Then, one day as he prayed, he forgot about himself as he prayed for the people to whom he would speak. He pictured their faces and remembered their pressures, their needs, their joys, and their sorrows. Before he stood to speak, he made a deliberate shift in approach. This time, rather than being anxious about delivering his sermon, and worrying about how well he performed, he focused on connecting these people whom he loved with the message God had given. Self-giving love replaced self-conscious fear. When he changed his way of looking at his task, there were positive consequences he never imagined possible.

Jesus said: "The eye is the lamp of the body. So, if your eye is healthy, your whole body will be full of light; but if your eye is unhealthy, your whole body will be full of darkness" (Matthew 6:22-23). Brother Stanley explained how the "eye" represents our "outlook" on life, or, the way we look at things. If we approach life asking, "How will this benefit me?" then our personality is darkened. Repentance (*metanoia*) is a shift in perspective. No longer preoccupied with how something will affect us, we are intentionally viewing the situation from a Kingdom perspective, asking, "What will honor and please him?" God's light infuses us. We are living from a new center (*How to Be a Transformed Person* [New York: Abingdon Press, 1951], p. 134).

When we experience the breadth of God's love and how it extends and applies in areas beyond what we had thought, it not only changes us, but also affects those around us as well. The other side is also true: what our faith community discovers and teaches us about the breadth of God's love is the soil in which we all grow.

(2) *The length of God's love.* Think of how far the love of God took Brother Stanley. He was raised in an ordinary home, received an ordinary education, and seemed to have rather

ordinary abilities; and yet look what happened when the love of Christ was at the center of his life.

Are you surprised at how far God has brought you? Are you amazed at how he redeems past mistakes, provides strength through others' love, shows you your gifts, and uses you to encourage or help other people?

When we are centered in love, God deploys us where he wills and provides for us along the way. "The LORD is your keeper," wrote the psalmist (Psalm 121:5). The Hebrew term for "to keep" can be translated "to guard" or "to watch over." The phrase conjures the picture of a vigilant sentry posted on an ancient city wall. What an encouragement to know that God constantly watches over us with undivided attention because we are precious to him.

People with a longitudinal experience of God's love are the spiritual mothers and fathers who have "known him who is from the beginning" (1 John 2:13 NIV). After years of experience they are convinced that God's grace truly *is* sufficient, his strength really *is* "made perfect in [our] weakness" (2 Corinthians 12:9 NIV). They have come to the conclusion that they actually can do "all things through [Christ]" as they rely on his strength (Philippians 4:13). They have arrived at a simple conclusion: I cannot make it without the Holy Spirit who works in me or apart from his Body that surrounds me.

(3) *The depths of God's love.* The fact that we are grounded in love does not mean that we automatically show it in healthy ways. In fact, the older we become, the more we are aware of our inner blockages and inabilities and our self-defeating and unhealthy patterns of relating to others. We are well aware that we have our "blind spots," where others can see things about us of which we are unaware. We also have the uneasy feeling that there are also regions of our subconscious, unknown to us and to others, that have a powerful negative influence over our motivation, relationships, and actions.

Brother Stanley loved to teach how God cleanses, consecrates, and coordinates the energy residing in our subconscious depths when we surrender to God. Brother Stanley explained that we do not have to continue as a divided self, but can embrace what the Holy Spirit is doing in us. "So if we surrender 'all we know'—the conscious mind—'and all we don't know'—the subconscious—then the Holy Spirit takes over areas in the subconscious which have hitherto been 'enemy territory' and now makes them friendly territory" (*A Song of Ascents*, p. 54).

This deep spiritual cleansing and healing is essential, but it does not eliminate human passions and instinctual needs. Brother Stanley observed how many Christians try to deal with those drives by suppressing them, as if they can gain control by willpower and block out certain thoughts or stifle unacceptable desires. Brother Stanley taught a much more healthy and helpful way.

The Christian approach, he explained, is to acknowledge our negative and troubling thoughts and, rather than despising ourselves for having them, to reframe them; and rather than attempting to block or "stuff" unacceptable impulses, to express them, but on a higher level.

For example, think of our innate human need to "belong." Liberated by surrender, we can now serve and love others, rather than being dominated by our need to "fit in," be liked, or have others' approval. The self, now dedicated to Christ, expresses itself as servant of all.

Here's another example: consider the implications for the energies of sex. Dedicated to God, sexual desire can become a creative energy for bearing children and expressing love and intimacy with one's mate; or sexual desire can be sublimated, channeled into inspiring and imaginative contributions, movements, projects, hopes, and souls. Emancipated, the powers of our sexual drives are set free, directed for love and service to Christ, and guided by watchful prayer (*A Song of Ascents*, p. 55).

The key to experiencing this integrating power of God's love in our inner depths is self-surrender. When we hand ourselves over to Christ, he reorients us. Now, rather than seeking our own satisfaction, we are living to serve Christ by showing his love for others. It is a decision we make, and one we must continue making.

In every devotional book he wrote, Stanley Jones supplied practical steps to help us tame the monsters and free the powers within us. Almost always his list of strategies would begin with the counsel that we honestly admit our need or struggle. He followed this by suggesting several practical and useful methods or approaches. The last step was almost always a fresh surrender to Christ. He always gave hope because he knew by experience that living in God's love results in substantial healing.

We experience the working of God's love in our depths, not only by the integrating and redirecting of our energies, but also by enriching our inner life so that it becomes a resource for good. When Jesus said, "The good person brings good things out of a good treasure" (Matthew 12:35), he seemed to be pointing in this direction. The inner storehouse of the subconscious, so troublesome to us because of its negative content, can also be an important ally. We can stock up on good things in the storehouse of the heart by daily adding to it good attitudes, thoughts, deeds, purposes, and victories, thus piling up reserves. Then, when temptation comes, or pressure, we come through because of our hidden resources (*A Song of Ascents*, p. 54).

As I think of some of the people I know who are experiencing God's inner healing and whose inner lives are becoming richer each year, I can't help thinking about the positive effects on those close to them.

- Destructive family patterns are stopped.
- Addictions are broken.
- Creative energies are released.
- Caring is their priority.
- They are becoming persons of peace.
- Honest about their own issues, they are realistic about their daily, or hourly, dependence upon the Spirit.
- God is shaping them into carriers of grace and healers of the souls of others.

(4) *The heights of God's love.* Stanley Jones is a wonderful example of one who demonstrates the power of God's love to help us

rise above our circumstances and to transcend those things that otherwise could overwhelm or undermine us. On December 8, 1971, after he had just completed a two-month evangelistic tour of Japan, he suffered a debilitating stroke that paralyzed the left side of his body and badly impaired his eyesight and his ability to speak. He was eighty-seven years old.

Months of rehabilitation followed. Physically there were slight improvements, but he was pragmatic about his limitations. He wanted to complete one last project, the manuscript for *The Divine Yes*. He finally achieved that goal, though not without the loving and skillful assistance of his daughter, Eunice, and his son-in-law, Jim Mathews. The book was published after his death in 1973.

The Divine Yes, as all the other books he wrote, was born out of human need. Brother Stanley knew that his own immediate need was also an ultimate human need: how can we possibly make it if we are stripped of practically everything? How can we overcome a "defeat" that seems utterly final?

He had written scores of books over the years, but in some ways his last may be the most eloquent and powerful. Weakened and suffering from the many complications of his stroke, he writes about his love of life, his realization that sickness and tragedy are malevolent intrusions into God's order, and his conviction that gloom and despair will not have the last word. He identifies with Jesus and the cross. He reflects about how Jesus took apparent "failure" and turned it into triumph, and how God uses the cross to overcome darkness and hate through light and love. Since God, in a great reversal, redeemed humanity through the cross, Brother Stanley determined that he could not fail. "You cannot defeat defeat. You cannot break brokenness," he wrote (*The Divine Yes* [Nashville: Abingdon Press, 1975], p. 25). He made up his mind that if he could not preach his messages, he would turn his life into one.

One of his final journal entries in December 1972 was made at the Sat-Tal Ashram, the community that was his spiritual home.

Now that I am in this crisis I face the question of living on crippled or calling it a day and accepting a passage to the other world. I am honestly indifferent as to which it shall be. I don't know what the future holds, but I know who holds it. I have tried for eighty-eight years (and in a few days it will be eighty-nine), and I have no need to live any more unless he decides. I have often said half jokingly that when I get to heaven, I will ask for twenty-four hours to see my friends, and then I shall go up to **him** and say, "Haven't you a world somewhere which has fallen people who need an evangelist like me? Please send me there." For I know no heaven beyond preaching the Gospel to people. That is heaven to me. It has been, is, and ever shall be heaven to me. (*The Divine Yes*, pp. 148–49)

QUESTIONS

1. What do you think of Brother Stanley's notion about the "conversion of our love"?
2. How has being in a faith community helped you discover more of God's love than you could have known by trying to go it alone?
3. Talk together about the way Brother Stanley understood and handled his great adversity.

VIII. Can I Really Become a Disciplined Christian?

> *I stayed for a week in the home of the president of a theological college. In saying good-bye he said something that rather startled me: "You are the most disciplined person I have ever seen. You don't waste a moment and you don't waste a word, and yet you are relaxed."*
> *The reason why I was startled was this: I didn't feel disciplined. To be told I was disciplined was something different from what I was telling myself: "You are free—and happy."* (A Song of Ascents)

Two words—freedom and discipline—Stanley Jones saw as Siamese twins. They "go together like the words and music of a song" (*A Song of Ascents* [Nashville: Abingdon Press, 1968], p. 296). At Dr. Jones's Sat-Tal Ashram in India, the motto on the walls is, "This is a place of freedom through discipline."

The Fresh Breeze of Liberation

Gene Peterson, as we called him during his college days at Seattle Pacific, was a runner. Early morning or late afternoon, he circled the track. He could be seen on campus with his running shoes. Come the track meets, he moved with astonishing speed.

Gene majored in English. He worked assiduously at developing writing skills. When, in later years, the name Eugene Peterson appeared on book jackets, his English professors recalled their student with pride.

In graduate school, he mastered both Hebrew and Greek and then taught the biblical languages in seminary. Later in the pastorate, he developed Bible studies with his church members and taught with marked enthusiasm. Wanting ever so much to help his people see the real meaning of Scripture, he began translating the Scriptures in everyday language, in modern English. The Bible study group got so interested in his fresh renderings that they couldn't even finish their coffee; they sat glued to the mimeographed pages on the study table.

Encouraged by the response to his God-inspired versions of Bible passages, he pressed on to translate more, first in the New Testament, later in the Old Testament. Today every Christian, and many a non-Christian, knows about *The Message*, designed, as Peterson says, so everyone can grasp the Word of God.

I have pondered the secret of our Seattle Pacific student becoming teacher, pastor, and translator. In reflection, I remember him developing public leadership and language skills when he served as student body president. Along with students, we professors listened to him in student chapels. He's "a comer," we all seemed to know.

Why? What dynamics drove him?

Was it a strong desire to succeed? Yes, without question. A love of language? Clearly. Devotion to his Lord? No debate. The thrill of discovery? A hearty yes. A bright mind coupled with a creative spirit? Evident to anyone around him. And God-gifted? The ultimate *yes*.

All this and more contributed to the dedicated service that characterizes Eugene Peterson. But somewhere along the time line of life, he set his will to master what he signed up for: competitive running, English, biblical languages, and writing. He put his shoulder to the wheel and pursued each challenge in turn. The result? Mastery and freedom to exercise what he had mastered.

Listen to Peterson's translation of verses about discipline. Proverbs 12:1: "If you love learning, you love the discipline that goes with it— / how shortsighted to refuse correction!" Hebrews 12:1: "Do you see what this means—all these pioneers who blazed the way, all these veterans cheering us on? It means we'd better get on with it. Strip down, start running—and never quit! No extra spiritual fat, no parasitic sins." Then the words of Hebrews 12:2: "Keep your eyes on *Jesus*, who both began and finished this race we're in. Study how he did it. Because he never lost sight of where he was headed—that exhilarating finish in and with God—he could put up with anything along the way: cross, shame, whatever. And now he's *there*, in the place of honor, right alongside God" (*Message*).

There you have Gene Peterson's theology of discipline, and he applied it to running as well as to writing, to pastoring, and to translating. Meet him today and you intuit the liberation, the happy freedom, of a disciplined man.

JESUS THE MODEL

Peterson's translation uncovers Jesus' secret: Jesus kept his eye on the goal and let nothing deter him. Not the cross, and not shame. His determination to redeem humankind determined in turn the nature of his disciplines.

Would Jesus have the sheer human strength to execute God's plan for his life? He stayed *physically fit*. He walked everywhere. He ate simply, no doubt following historic Jewish dietary patterns. He slept. He modeled a healthy lifestyle.

Could he stay in tune with God's Spirit, Director of his life? Note Jesus' life of *prayer*: he taught his disciples the Lord's Prayer (Matthew 6:9-13). He prayed one of the great prayers of all time, recorded in John 17:1-26. His prayer of agony in the Garden (Luke 22:39-46) identifies with suffering the world over.

Did he master the *Scriptures*? Clearly he knew the Old Testament, for virtually everything he said reflected intimate knowledge of it. More, he knew how to interpret it in light of his messiahship.

Could he relate with *social skill*? Jesus models friendship (for example, his friendship with Martha, Mary, and Lazarus), authoritative leadership (he gave superb direction to the disciples), and resistance to evil (note his forthright dealings with the Pharisees—[Matthew 23] and with authorities at his trial—[Matthew 26–27]). He spoke truth with love (for example, the woman of Samaria in John 4).

Would he *fast*? The forty days in the wilderness (Matthew 4:2) documents the answer. And he tells us what attitude to embrace when we fast (Matthew 6:16).

Did he *master communication*? Notice the Sermon on the Mount (Matthew 5–7), observe his teaching skill in asking questions (for example, in Matthew 7:9-10), and look at the pictures called parables (for example, in Matthew 13).

What about a *pure life*? Read his strong statements about integrity (see Matthew 5:6 on righteousness), sincerity (see what he says about the heart in Matthew 5:8), and sexual relationships (see Matthew 5:27-30).

Did he sense the need for *fellowship*? Note his powerful words in Matthew 18:19-20: "When two of you get together on anything at all on earth and make a prayer of it, my Father in heaven goes into action. And when two or three of you are together because of me, you can be sure that I'll be there" (*Message*).

Could he embrace *sacrifice*? Who can doubt the answer when reading what he said about persecution (Matthew 5:10-12) and looking at the passion narratives and the story of the cross?

What about *compassion*? He healed people nonstop (for example, the woman who had a spirit of infirmity for eighteen years in Luke 13:10ff). The narratives in Luke 15 on the lost sheep, the lost coin, and the lost son, have to be some of the great compassion stories of all time.

And *service*? Everyone knows the classic text, "The Son of Man came not to be served but to serve, and to give his life a ransom for many" (Matthew 20:28). He followed his own preaching with astonishing exactness, thus teaching us how to give ourselves to others in responsible service.

How about a *simple lifestyle*? Jesus clearly lived by Matthew 6:24: "No one can serve two masters; for a slave will either hate the one and love the other, or be devoted to the one and despise the other. You cannot serve God and wealth."

Could he get away by himself or with a select few for *solitude and silence?* Note passages that answer that question: In Matthew 14:23, we're told he left the crowds and went to a mountain by himself to pray. Early in the morning, he got up to pray in a deserted place (Mark 1:35). Mark 6:31 paints a vivid picture: "Come away to a deserted place all by yourselves and rest a while." Mark 9:2 says Jesus took Peter, James, and John to a high mountain by themselves. Luke 4:42 tells us of his quiet time at daybreak. Luke 6:12 informs us that he spent a night in prayer.

What about *surrender?* Matthew 6:10, part of our Lord's Prayer, gives us the basic answer: "Your kingdom come. / Your will be done, on earth as it is in heaven." And remind yourself of the poignant prayer, "My Father, if it is possible, let this cup pass from me; yet not what I want but what you want" (Matthew 26:39).

Worship too? His teaching comes clear in Matthew 4:10, the declaration to the devil, "Worship the Lord your God, and only him. Serve him with absolute single-heartedness" (*Message*).

A KEY DISCIPLINE: SURRENDER

Work assiduously at mastery, and when it comes, enjoy the freedom in exercising skills and disciplines. But a crucial question remains: Where does the motivation to master come from?

The answer to that finds its locus in genuine surrender. Catherine Marshall tells about her stepdaughter's fight to keep from losing her retainer. The young girl had gone to the orthodontist to have her teeth straightened. The dentist put bands on her teeth; and when, after some months, that painful part of the process came to an end, the doctor made her a retainer to hold the teeth in place until fixed for life. She was to wear the device between meals and while sleeping. But she had a terrible time remembering to put it in her mouth; worse, she would forget where she put it. One day, while taking a trip with Catherine, she got off the train, leaving the retainer behind her in the ladies room.

She lost the retainer over and again, and as many parents know, replacing it was costly. Catherine asked her daughter to pray with her several nights in a row—pray until the matter lodged firmly in her mind, until, in fact, she surrendered to keeping track of the retainer.

It worked. The teenager continued through the long process, years actually, of wearing the mouthpiece until her teeth were right.

That story becomes a parable for fixing our spiritual disciplines. As a listening minister, I have heard a lot of anxiety about the quiet time—prayer, Scripture, devotional reading. *I say I will have prayer time and scripture reading, but I forget. Or I thought I had willed this thing, but the activities of life crowd in and I have lived another day without time with the Lord.*

Once genuine surrender to the Helper, the Holy Spirit, becomes reality, one practices the disciplines with joy. Adoring love of God comes naturally, and God responds with his presence.

Your Own Assigned Program

First, know that God has an assignment just for you. He does not want you to adopt someone else's devotional and lifestyle pattern; it must be yours. God has a program tailor-made for you.

How do you find that program? You could begin by looking at a framework for the practice of Christian disciplines. Take, for example, John Wesley's five means of grace. You could list the five, making notes to yourself under each, such as the following:

PRAYER

Journaling—List concerns and record answers to prayer.

Timing—Early morning? Mid-day? Evening?

Prayer partner— God assigns partners. Could this be a mentor?

Prayer chain—Should I volunteer at my church?

SCRIPTURE

Daily—Scripture study during my quiet time? After all, prayer and God's Word go together, else my prayers turn selfish.

How will I savor discoveries? Make notes in my journal? Mark my study Bible?

Would devotional readings, in books or on a website, enrich my understanding of Scripture?

What commentaries speak to me?

How can I put into practice what I find in the Bible?

FASTING

John Wesley fasted regularly. Does God call me to fast weekly? Monthly? When I sense the need?

What ways should I fast? From meals? From TV? From talk? From sweets? At certain times of the year (Lent, for example)?

Fasting from food reminds me of dietary concerns. Am I honoring my body as the temple of God's Spirit? And this reminds me of physical fitness. Do I exercise?

EUCHARIST

The eighteenth-century Wesleyan movement was a revival of Holy Communion as well as of conversion and nurture. The Wesleys published an entire hymnbook called *Hymns on the Lord's Supper*.

Do I take Holy Communion regularly? Often enough?

When I take the bread and the cup, do I refresh my awareness of the presence of Christ?

Before taking the Eucharist, do I prepare adequately?

Do I carry away from the Table of the Lord the sense of his presence into my daily life?

CONFERENCE

John Wesley believed fellowship—getting together with like-minded godly people—nurtured the soul.

So I can ask myself crucial questions:

Do I attend public worship regularly? And with a receptive heart?

Do I participate in group prayer? A regular prayer meeting? Small or church-wide? With my family?

Do I take advantage of retreat opportunities?

Do Christian conferences find a place on my calendar? Both learning and inspiration feed me at such events.

You could take another approach to discovering your program: simply pray through the twelve disciplines used in Richard Foster's writings. Ask, "Lord, how do you want me to relate to these twelve? Guide me to your assigned program."

THE INWARD DISCIPLINES
1. Meditation
2. Prayer
3. Fasting
4. Study

THE OUTWARD DISCIPLINES
   5. Simplicity
   6. Solitude
   7. Submission
   8. Service

THE CORPORATE DISCIPLINES
   9. Confession
   10. Worship
   11. Guidance
   12. Celebration

You can read about these disciplines in Richard Foster's *Celebration of Discipline: The Path to Spiritual Growth*, rev. ed. (San Francisco: Harper & Row, 1988). You may also want to have a look at Dallas Willard's *The Spirit of the Disciplines: Understanding How God Changes Lives* (San Francisco: Harper & Row, 1988), and read Stanley Jones's delightful chapter "I Sing of Freedom and Discipline" in *A Song of Ascents*.

GETTING A WHOLESOME PERSPECTIVE ON DISCIPLINES

Avoiding legalism. Jesus had quite a lot to say about the Pharisees tending to the minutia of the law but missing its purpose (Matthew 23). A self-enforced "must" to doing disciplines will only result in inner conflict. During Augustine's promiscuous years, he cried to the Lord in self-inflicted flagellation: "Lord, You have to heal me of lust." This only hammered lust into Augustine's brain all the more. Once Augustine "let go and let God," he found release, freedom, and disciplined control over his sexual desires.

Seeing the essentiality of discipline. Stanley Jones reasoned, "If there is no discipline in a song, going from one harmonious note to another, there is no freedom to sing" (*A Song of Ascents*, p. 296). Jesus made the same kind of observation: "Enter by the narrow gate; for the gate is wide and the way is easy, that leads to destruction, and those who enter by it are many. For the gate is narrow and the way is hard, that leads to life, and those who find it are few" (Matthew 7:13-14 RSV). Peterson's translation underscores with fresh vividness this lifestyle law: "Don't look for shortcuts to God. The market is flooded with surefire, easygoing formulas for a successful life that can be practiced in your spare time. Don't fall for that stuff, even though crowds of people do. The way to life—to God!—is vigorous and requires total attention" (*Message*).

Learning the true secret of self-fulfillment. The "Me" generation says "I want to do my thing." What's the problem with that? Only God can bring us to fulfillment. When we take charge of our lives, pretending we are God, we make choices that inevitably lead to bad results. George Matheson in 1980 captured the truly workable life in this great hymn:

> Make me a captive, Lord,
> and then I shall be free.
> Force me to render up my sword,
> and I shall conqueror be.
> I sink in life's alarms
> when by myself I stand;
> imprison me within thine arms,
> and strong shall be my hand.

The last verse sums it all up:

> My will is not my own
> till thou hast made it thine;
> if it would reach a monarch's throne,
> it must its crown resign.
> It only stands unbent
> amid the clashing strife,
> when on thy bosom it has leant
> and found in thee its life.
>   ("Make Me a Captive, Lord," 1890)

Stanley Jones again: "The deepest conviction of my life is this: Self-surrender is the way to self-expression. You realize yourself only as you renounce yourself. You find God when you renounce yourself as God. The self is trying to play God, trying to organize life around itself as God, and it simply doesn't work.... You have to lose your life to find it" (*A Song of Ascents*, p. 297).

Inviting the devotional classics into your mind and heart. Read the great writers and they will reveal their secrets in astonishing and often surprising ways. Start with two leading anthologies:

Richard J. Foster and James Bryan Smith, eds. *Devotional Classics: Selected Readings for Individuals and Groups*. San Francisco: HarperSanFrancisco, 1990.

Richard J. Foster and Emilie Griffin, eds. *Spiritual Classics: Selected Readings for Individuals and Groups on the Twelve Spiritual Disciplines*. San Francisco: HarperSanFrancisco, 2000.

Then select, say, five classics to read, perhaps these:

Thomas à Kempis, *Imitation of Christ*.
Brother Lawrence, *The Practice of the Presence of Christ*.
Thomas R. Kelly, *A Testament of Devotion*.
Stanley Jones, *Abundant Living*.
Hannah Whitall Smith, *The Christian's Secret of the Happy Life*.

Throughout your life, discover rich spiritual formation resources and invite the writers to play a significant role in your growth. Read the classics slowly, letting them take hold of you, permitting insights to filter down into your subconscious mind.

Coming to grips with time. Our overly busy culture tends to control time, but Christians by God's help must control their own time. Once we are surrendered to God's control, he shows us how to use time.

Two Greek words enrich our perspective on time. *Chronos* means just what it looks like—chronology—and defines calendar or clock time. The days unfold moment by moment in measured and predictable sequence.

The New Testament uses not only *chronos* but also *kairos*, God's time. The Messiah, the Bible teaches, came in *kairos*, God's appointed time. God answers prayer like this, though human beings would very much like him to answer by clock and calendar—right now! In developing discipline, we must use chronological time (*chronos*) and also respond to God at his special times (*kairos*).

Once in awhile I meet someone who does not require, for spiritual health maintenance, regular times of prayer, study, and meditation. But the counsel of most spiritual leaders holds true: after receiving Christ as Savior and experiencing the baptism of the Holy Spirit, no practice proves more rewarding to ourselves and others than observing the quiet time. Regularity makes its significant contribution toward making stable Christians. Have you noticed that people who say they do not need a regular quiet time tend to go paralytic in crisis and make poor choices?

So prayerfully determine your regular time with the Lord. On occasion something will disrupt it. Refuse the legalism that creates a barrier between you and the demands of others. Be flexible, yet respect the necessity of regularity. Seasoned Christians know their life goes up or down depending on prayer time. God uses prayer not only to grow us, but also to give us energy for our work and life.

But God also has his special timing. *Kairos* moments may come during your regular quiet time: during a grand moment of insight ("Oh! So that's the way life works"); during a burdensome prayer for someone or a situation; or when you find a solution to a problem. Again, a *kairos* moment may awaken you in the night to intercede for someone specifically or for some cause. At other times, God calls us to intercede for an unknown person or concern; you only know you must pray in a spirit of submission to his *kairos* call.

Learning to listen. Patiently cultivate your skill in detecting God's Voice. Stanley Jones called this the Inner Voice. Once you have sorted out the foreign voices (rationalizations and unbiblical, untested impressions) from the Voice, *ah ha* moments come. Creative solutions dawn.

Quietly sitting with the open Bible, interceding for those on your prayer list, lifting praises to God—these quiet activities lend themselves to listening. With his Voice comes peace, strength for the day, and that sense of well-being that characterizes released and joyful Christians.

QUESTIONS

1. How do you see God fitting into the spiritual disciplines? Does he initiate the call? Grace you with ability to respond? Embrace you with his presence as you lift heartfelt thanksgiving for his call?

2. Have I definitely surrendered myself to Jesus, thus making possible the life of discipline? Take your time answering this question. Let the Spirit of God invade your own spirit, allowing him to bring your surrender full circle.

3. What does God assign me? A pattern? Time for silence and study? When? In answering these questions, give the Spirit leisure to make clear his plan. Expect changes in that plan over time and as you mature in him.

4. See the larger picture of the disciplined life. To live in un-Kingdom ways is to lose both the Kingdom and yourself, observes Dr. Jones over and again (*Abundant Living* [New York: Abingdon-Cokesbury Press, 1942], pp. 190ff, the section on the Kingdom). Christian discipline is a lifestyle, influencing family, business, interpersonal relationships—the whole of life.

5. How will you handle the temptations to renege on the disciplined life? Temptations

come in many packages: rationalization ("I don't really have time"), self-preoccupation (prayer easily becomes a self-absorbed activity), and compromising on morals (money, power plays, and sex). Will a fresh look at the whole armor of God passage (Ephesians 6:10-20) help? Notice verse 10: strength to fight is the Lord himself—*he*, with your consent, answers the threat of temptation.

6. I ask you the question I ask myself: Do I see myself growing in comprehension of the enormous value of soul development? If you want to consciously move more in that direction, see, for example, Joseph Pearce's *Solzhenitsyn: A Soul in Exile* (Grand Rapids: Baker Book House, 1999). Or spend time with a great devotional anthology such as John W. Doberstein's *Minister's Prayer Book: An Order of Prayers and Readings* (Philadelphia: Fortress Press, 1986).

IX. DOES GOD GUIDE US?

Does God guide us? Strange if he didn't. (A Song of Ascents)

Yes, God guides us. Stanley Jones sees the Holy Spirit guiding us in at least five ways: (1) by the life, character, and teaching of Christ; (2) by the counsel of good people; (3) by an opening Providence; (4) by heightened moral intelligence; and (5) by the Inner Voice (*A Song of Ascents*, pp. 188–90). The five overlap and together provide a holistic approach to guidance. God expects us to use all of our resources to discern his will.

But how do we get ready to let God guide us?

GUIDANCE READINESS

We are creatures of habit, and to break out of habits of self-direction into the liberated lifestyle of openness to God's will requires both understanding and willingness on our part.

Stanley Jones tells of a woman who had lived in the "foul, heavy air of the slums of New York." She became physically ill when visiting the country with its clean, fresh air. "Her lungs had become so accustomed to unnatural foulness that natural freshness was unnatural!" Then Brother Stanley tells of the South American city in which a new market, clean and sanitary with nicely tiled floors and walls, turned one woman off: "That market is so clean it makes me sick. It is just like a hospital" (*Abundant Living* [New York: Abingdon-Cokesbury Press, 1942], p. 211).

These pictures serve as a metaphor of our hesitation to break out of our ways into God's way, out of self-direction to

God-direction. Jones writes forthrightly about our reluctance: "Christ ... sees us with our unworkable ways of life, running into roads with dead ends, ending in frustration and futility, losing our means of living, and our lives themselves, and He says again: 'Seek ye first the kingdom of God.... And all these things shall be added unto you.' But we are seeking other things first, and all these things are being subtracted from us" (ibid.).

What is the first step, then, toward openness to guidance? It is facing our stubbornness, the wall we create against listening and learning. As a professor for half a century, I have often had a private laugh about students who pay tuition and invest time, but put up barriers to learning. That incongruous behavior not only makes me laugh, but also brings tears to my eyes. I have gently but firmly counseled students to look at their hesitation to learn. Thankfully, most go through a major attitude change, now saying, "I'm eager to learn," thus turning their backs firmly against the posture that declares, "Don't try to tell me something."

Find the grand clue to guidance readiness in the time-honored verses of Proverbs 3:

> Trust in the LORD with all your heart,
> and do not rely on your own insight.
> In all your ways acknowledge him,
> and he will make straight your paths. (vv. 5-6)

THE LIFE, CHARACTER, AND TEACHING OF CHRIST

Jesus declares, "I am the way, and the truth, and the life" (John 14:6). So Jesus offers himself as our guide to truth and to life itself, and his sheep follow him (John 10). How can we lose our way if we follow the Way?

But, "God cannot guide us in any way that would contradict the character of Jesus" (*A Song of Ascents*, p. 188). A young lady said, "I'm sleeping with my boyfriend," then asked, "That's OK, isn't it?" My reply: "Do you find an OK for your behavior in the New Testament?" She turned silent.

Jesus not only models but also summarizes the biblical stance on guidance in the Sermon on the Mount (Matthew 5–7). Interestingly, Jesus begins the sermon with a summary of the basic principle of guidance; that summary we call the Beatitudes. The Beatitudes tell us that the meek, the seeking, the contented, the humble, those hungering after God, those cooperating with God, the committed—in other words, people genuinely looking to God as their Leader—hear from God! Especially the down-and-outers and the persecuted who follow God, enjoy his guiding presence.

Jesus tells us that God's followers are salt and light in this evil world; they show, by example, how to live the guided life. And what does that exemplary life look like? True followers

- Commit no murder (Matthew 5:21-26)
- Refuse adultery and unlawful divorce (Matthew 5:27-32)
- Stand by their promises (Matthew 5:33-37)
- Love even their enemies (Matthew 5:38-48)
- Say no to duplicity (Matthew 6:1-4)
- Pray with simplicity (Matthew 6:5-18)
- Worship God by the way they live (Matthew 6:19-34)
- Relate to people with integrity (Matthew 7:1-12)
- Listen to God, not to false prophets (Matthew 7:13-29)

Jesus himself inspires us to live with this system of guidance, and he lived by his own preaching, by messages he heard from his heavenly Father.

THE COUNSEL OF GOOD PEOPLE

Guidance through a few good people. This morning I visited with Marilyn, Director of Spouse Ministries at my seminary. She created a Board of Wisdom, women who come to her office to listen to her problems and pray with her. In this seeking atmosphere,

Marilyn hears divine solutions. "I can't handle the stickler problems by myself; I must find guidance in community," she declares.

Marilyn's conviction reminds us of the guidance given to the good people in Acts 14:23: "Paul and Barnabas handpicked leaders in each church. After praying—their prayers intensified by fasting—they presented these new leaders to the Master to whom they had entrusted their lives" (*Message*).

Listeners hear. Hearers act. People who act get Kingdom work done. Clearly, Jesus promised his children guidance from the Father: "Truly I tell you, if two of you agree on earth about anything you ask, it will be done for you by my Father in heaven. For where two or three are gathered in my name, I am there among them" (Matthew 18:19-20).

Guidance through counselors, unwitting guides, and mentors. God uses Christian counselors to help us find our way. When in grade school and high school, Robert suffered emotionally because of nasty comments and social isolation brought on by a bright mind and an overweight body. Fortunately this did not deter him from college and graduate school. He earned a degree in jurisprudence and enjoys a good job in the professional world. But the trauma of early childhood made therapy necessary. The counselor took him by the hand, as it were, guided him out of the maze of conflicted emotions, and helped him identify himself. No wonder he celebrated newfound freedom!

Robert's happy story could be repeated a thousand times. Fortunately, counselors with sound biblical orientation have put out their shingles in many places. They are some of God's appointed guides.

Most of us do not need that kind of intensive guidance; we do need answers to the daily and unrelenting challenges of life: the next step in vocation, the family problem, the financial stress, the interpersonal issues. Often God provides answers for us through his faithful followers. Your pastor says something in a sermon, a hymn writer communicates to the heart of a concern, a passing comment from a coworker issued in a moment of insight and resolution. Alert, listening Christians get help, sometimes at the most unexpected moments.

And what about mentors? At some point in our lives, most of us need mentors. Often those guides do not know they are mentors; they simply live and talk, work and serve in such a way that they tell us by their very lives where to find answers and how to solve problems. Other mentors—gifted consultants—know by experience and training how to help us. They make themselves open to appointments and ordered conversation about the issues of our lives and guide us along the road to maturity. You will want to pray and think through the advisability of seeking out an experienced mentor.

AN OPENING PROVIDENCE

Often I have found that Providence comes to my rescue in the midst of a challenge. What on earth can I do? I ask. Better to ask, "What plan does God have for solving my problem?" Once I have surrendered the issue totally to God, I begin to see him at work. He always works in his own time (*kairos*) and frequently by surprise. Anticipated solutions rarely materialize; in fact, the solution may be so surprising that it blinds me at first from seeing the answer. More, his answers may well open doors to Kingdom-building activity, making the Providence a call to ministry.

Stanley Jones loved the idea of hunting black buck in India. As a young missionary he discovered his district richly populated by deer; so why not, on his rounds of village visits, enjoy sport along with contacting people for Christ? What happened came as a complete surprise: "I shot eighteen times at . . . [black bucks] and never hit one! Bad marksman? No, as a youth I was the best marksman in our crowd." Providence stepped in: "I had the feeling that God was making me miss. So I took the gun home and sold it, concluding that God had not called me to be a hunter, but an evangelist." Stanley Jones saw more to the Providence: "I might have been crippled by a secondary success. Many a woman, finding she has beauty, soon finds she has nothing else. The secondary success of beauty makes her neglect the primary facts of intelligence and soul and usefulness" (*Victorious Living* [New York: Abingdon Press, 1936], p. 256).

The theology of providential guidance never ceases to fascinate me. God, it seems, comes up on our blind side and surprises us. Surely the whole idea of surprise originates in the heart of God. Built in his image, we have surprise parties with candles, speeches, and balloons, and we relish the sheer joy of the fulfillment surprise brings.

Yet sometimes God's providential guidance does not have the overtones of joy, at least for the moment. When he guides, we follow, even if for the time being the result seems negative. In the long haul, God may reveal his solution, demonstrating he really does guide all along the way. So a rebellious son gets angry at parental guidance, an employee resents a change in assignment, a pastor simply cannot see why the bishop appointed him or her to *this* church. Hang in there, even over the years, and watch God at work. Hang in there, too, with your openness to direction, and experience the peace of God that passes all understanding. Even if the revelation of his will never comes on the screen of your understanding, you have the deep satisfaction of knowing you followed God's plan.

HEIGHTENED MORAL INTELLIGENCE

In another place Brother Stanley calls moral intelligence "enlightened" intelligence (*Victorious Living*, p. 257). The two intelligences, moral and enlightened, come together in Eugene Peterson's translation of Hebrews 5:11-14:

> I have a lot more to say about this, but it is hard to get it across to you since you've picked up this bad habit of not listening. By this time you ought to be teachers yourselves, yet here I find you need someone to sit down with you and go over the basics on God again, starting from square one—baby's milk, when you should have been on solid food long ago! Milk is for beginners, inexperienced in God's ways; solid food is for

the mature, who have some practice in telling right from wrong. (*Message*)

We have all noticed the harm done to overprotected children in their growing-up years. Twenty-somethings, even thirty-somethings, still on milk, come up against nasty turns in life but do not know how to handle them. Evaluation, discernment, and coping skills lie dormant. In the face of challenges, some go paralytic, opting out of the workplace; others escape into sex, alcohol, drugs, and other addictions; still others wrestle with inner demons. (A splendid article on the phenomenon of overprotection is "Against Eternal Youth" by Frederica Mathewes-Green, in *First Things* [August/September 2005]: pp. 9–11.)

We can guide rather than override our children, freeing them to mature and to come to grips with the realities of life. All of us, whether brought up in a learning atmosphere or not, can strengthen our capacity to cope by nourishing the impulse to advance in knowledge. We can do this by reading, travelling, associating with alert people, asking penetrating questions, watching the news (with a critical eye), embracing the challenges and experiences of life, and studying the scriptures.

Discernment defines the enlightened intellect. The Bible has some pointed observations about discernment. Isaiah 27:11 says people without discernment will not enjoy the compassion and favor of God. In Philippians 1:9, Paul prays that his people will abound in knowledge and "all discernment" (RSV). Words such as *perception, insight, awareness,* and *clear-eyed* help us grasp what the Bible means by discernment.

The ability to discern grows by exercising good sense. My wife and I have puzzled over the news about the loss of a beautiful young woman on one of the islands in the Caribbean. She had joined a group of teens celebrating their high school graduation. No one knows what happened to her; she just disappeared. Common sense would indicate the need for an effective buddy system (her roommate did not act as a buddy), staying away from strangers (she spent time with a perfect stranger the night of her disappearance), monitoring alcohol consumption (she and her friends got drunk), and adult supervision (news reports indicated no adults were with the group of youth). What happened to planning, to the use of intelligence, to sense? Evidently common sense is not so common.

Notice the way the early church exercised common sense. For example, Acts 6:2-4 shows the apostles "using their heads" about the division of labor: "So the Twelve called a meeting of the disciples. They said, 'It wouldn't be right for us to abandon our responsibilities for preaching and teaching the Word of God to help with the care of the poor. So, friends, choose seven men from among you whom everyone trusts, men full of the Holy Spirit and good sense, and we'll assign them this task. Meanwhile, we'll stick to our assigned tasks of prayer and speaking God's Word'" (*Message*).

Preparation for marriage signals a major need for discernment. Today, with marriage preparation programs widely available, couples enjoy opportunities to ask questions, address issues, learn conflict management skills, and obtain personality profiles to learn about possible compatibility.

Our age, replete with self-assessment instruments—vocational surveys, college preparation guides, marriage readiness programs, what have you—provides a wealth of possibilities for discernment enrichment.

THE INNER VOICE

The Inner Voice "is the Spirit of God speaking to one directly and authentically" (*Victorious Living*, p. 260). That Voice helps us discern right from wrong, gives counsel for decision-making, shows ways to handle dilemmas, indicates what tasks to take up or leave untouched, and points to prayer concerns. But how can we distinguish the subconscious from the Voice of God? "Perhaps the rough distinction is this: The voice of the subconscious argues with you, tries to convince you; but the inner voice of God does not argue, does not try to convince you. It just speaks and it is self-authenticating. It has the feel of the voice of God within it. 'The sheep follow him: for they know his voice'" (*A Song of Ascents*, p. 190).

We need to use *all* the means of guidance, not exclusively the Inner Voice. Have you noticed that people who always say, "The Lord told me," often rationalize? Psychologists call this "spiritualizing." The Voice of God becomes not the Spirit of God but the spirit of self and often unreality. Your own voice, left to itself, can misguide you.

But when the Inner Voice speaks, we know it because of the ring of authenticity. Often the Spirit speaks when we least expect him to speak, surprising us with insight, direction, confirmation, peace, and comfort. In this God shows himself gracious, for he skirts our emotional involvements that often point us, sometimes rather convincingly, in a wrong direction. God works in the context of his will, in the context of reality, and in the context of Kingdom perspective.

The direction of the Spirit dominated the early church. Notice the Voice of the Spirit to Peter in the great racial breakthrough chapter, Acts 10: "The Spirit whispered to him, 'Three men are knocking at the door looking for you. Get down there and go with them. Don't ask any questions. I sent them to get you.'" Observe Peter's response to the Spirit: "Peter went down and said to the men, 'I think I'm the man you're looking for. What's up?'" The rest of the story shows the fulfillment of God's guidance: "They said, 'Captain Cornelius, a God-fearing man well-known for his fair play—ask any Jew in this part of the country—was commanded by a holy angel to get you and bring you to his house so he could hear what you had to say.' Peter invited them in and made them feel at home" (vv. 20-23, *Message*).

Someone suggested changing the name of *The Acts of the Apostles* to *The Acts of the Holy Spirit* because of the extraordinary presence of the Guide in this New Testament book. Acts 16:6-8 illustrates this: "They went to Phrygia, and then on through the region of Galatia. Their plan was to turn west into Asia province, but the Holy Spirit blocked that route. So they went to Mysia and tried to go north to Bithynia, but the Spirit of Jesus wouldn't let them go there either. Proceeding on through Mysia, they went down to the seaport Troas" (*Message*). Note the fruit of that direction: "When I arrived in Troas to proclaim the Message of the Messiah, I found the place wide open: God had opened the door; all I had to do was walk through it" (2 Corinthians 2:12 *Message*).

The Spirit of God is the Spirit of Jesus in the book of Acts. "This gives the key by which we can discern the Voice of the Spirit—does that Voice appeal according to what we have seen in Christ? If so, I accept it. If not, I question it" (*Victorious Living*, p. 261).

Sometimes the Inner Voice does not communicate, even when you need an answer. Then do nothing until you get the guidance you need. To act too quickly may prove wrong, even disastrous. Notice in Acts 10 that Peter did not respond immediately; he puzzled, thought, prayed, and engaged in inner dialog. Only when the Spirit spoke did he act.

This whole business of waiting proves a crucial indicator of spirituality. Brother Stanley observes, "The difference in the spiritual lives of people is what they do with the spare moment. Some waste it—and themselves with it. Others gather it up and make it contribute." Then he tells a remarkable story to illustrate his point:

> In college I had to give a talk on missions, became burdened that something be done about it, and as I had a few moments before the beginning of the meeting, I stepped into a room and prayed, "O God, give me a missionary from this meeting. I'll not go in until I am assured that someone will go." The answer came, "Take one, according to your faith be it unto you." "I will," I replied, and went into the room with an inner assurance. From that moment I was gripped. I was the missionary! I had prayed myself into it. Pray and then put yourself in the way of being guided to answer that prayer. (*Victorious Living*, p. 265)

A CONCLUDING WORD ABOUT GUIDANCE

The sovereign God guides us continuously; in fact, most of the time we go about our life and work without much thought of guidance. God intends us to live like that. John Baillie's *Diary of Private Prayer* (London: Oxford University Press, 1936; reprinted many times) reminds us of God's ever-guiding presence, not only during waking hours, but even at the close of the day and in sleep.

We can work too hard at seeking God's will. While all aspects of the spiritual life call for incarnational involvement—the human and the divine working together—most of the work of guidance comes from God himself. Fussily trying to find his will, straining to determine it, goes contrary to the Bible's clear teaching about living in the context of God's offered rest.

> Gracious is the LORD, and righteous;
>> our God is merciful.
> The LORD protects the simple;
>> when I was brought low, he saved me.
> Return, O my soul, to your rest,
>> for the LORD has dealt bountifully with you.
>> (Psalm 116:5-7)

Notice the spirit of unfettered calm in Psalm 23—green pastures, still waters.

Do you remember the old saying, "Let go and let God"? There's the secret. Difficult in crisis? Of course. Possible in the power of his Spirit? Certainly.

QUESTIONS

1. You may wish to begin collecting a body of literature on guidance. Why not begin with Richard J. Foster and Emilie Griffin, *Spiritual Classics: Selected Readings for Individuals and Groups on the Twelve Spiritual Disciplines* (San Francisco: HarperSanFrancisco, 2000), the section on guidance, pp. 277ff. Add to that Richard Foster's *Celebration of Discipline: The*

Path to Spiritual Growth (San Francisco: Harper & Row, 1978), chapter 12, "Guidance," pp. 150ff. You could also look at the guidance scripture references in *The Renovaré Spiritual Formation Bible* edited by Richard J. Foster (San Francisco: HarperSanFrancisco, 2005, pp. 2300–2301).

2. Give some thought to how you seek guidance in crisis. You might wish to write out a personal experience; you could use your journal for this.

3. When God seems not to speak, do you find the challenge of patiently waiting disconcerting or an opportunity to pray and ponder? Perhaps both?

4. Do you have friends who could help you discern God's will?

5. Have you given thought to asking a mature Christian to mentor you?

EPILOGUE

"I am a Christian in the making."(E. Stanley Jones's oft-repeated affirmation and confession)

During Brother Stanley's last years, he quoted over and again 2 Corinthians 3:18: "And we all, with unveiled face, beholding the glory of the Lord, are being changed into his likeness from one degree of glory to another; for this comes from the Lord who is the Spirit" (RSV). That passage communicates Dr. Jones's deep conviction that God's Spirit continues to grow us to our last breath.

The seventeenth-century English theologian John Owen believed that. He observed that "a continual view of the glory of Christ will have the blessed effect of changing us more and more into the likeness of Christ." Owen went on to say, "Perhaps other ways and means have failed to make us Christlike." Then he challenges, "Let us put this way to the test." (*The Glory of Christ* [London: Grace Publications Trust, 1987], p. 86.)

Stanley Jones did indeed test this Spirit-led way of growing in Christ. In fact, he defined spiritual formation as "beholding the glory of the Lord"—getting ever closer to Christ, living in his Word, day by day enriching one's knowledge of who he is, seeing God in his children and in the creation—anything and everything that brings honor to his name. The result? "Being changed into his likeness."

Brother Stanley set a good example. Ongoing transformation into the image of God shows itself in the themes of each of the nine chapters in our book.

Transformation? Yes! Conversion and baptism begin the process. As we see ever more clearly the grandeur of God's salvation in his Son, we grow more and more like the Transformer.

Abundant living? Yes! Liberty in Christ begins with what John Wesley called Perfect Love. That love grows right through conflicts and challenges, as we keep our eyes on Jesus. More, he sent the Paraclete, the Holy Spirit, the One alongside us.

Christian community? Yes! Unity develops as we focus on the Unifier, Jesus himself.

Healing? Yes! Christ himself is the Healer. Savior means Healer. To see him healing in the Gospels and in the lives of our people inspires our own faith.

Power in preaching? Yes! The radiant Christ paints his picture on the mind of the proclaimer, and in turn the people sense the effect of the gospel.

Joy in this world? Yes! Jesus himself is the Source of that Joy, through the presence of his Spirit.

A Christian in the making? Yes! The Spirit of Jesus prepares us for growth, and he will not fail the devout seeker.

Discipline? Yes! One close look at the Christ turns us to meditation, prayer, and ongoing formation.

Guidance? Yes! With him at the center, we hear the Inner Voice, listen to counsel, find help in worship, see direction in scripture.

The New Revised Standard version of 2 Corinthians 3:18, with its mirror figure, enriches our understanding of the spiritual formation to which God calls us: "And all of us, with unveiled faces, seeing the glory of the Lord as though reflected in a mirror, are being transformed into the same image from one degree of glory to another; for this comes from the Lord, the Spirit."